Girl in the Dark

DOUBLEDAY

New York   London   Toronto   Sydney   Auckland

Girl in the Dark

A MEMOIR

Anna Lyndsey

All events related in *Girl in the Dark* are factual. The author is using a pen name and has changed identifying details of people in the book to protect the privacy of her family, friends and associates. Conversations have been reconstructed from memory. See also the Author's Note on page 251.

All rights reserved. Published in the United States by Doubleday, a division of Random House LLC, New York, and in Canada by Random House of Canada Limited, Toronto, Penguin Random House companies.

www.doubleday.com

Published simultaneously in Great Britain by Bloomsbury, London.

DOUBLEDAY and the portrayal of an anchor with a dolphin are registered trademarks of Random House LLC.

Book design by Maria Carella
Jacket design by Emily Mahon
Case photograph © Stocktrek/Getty Images

Library of Congress Cataloging-in-Publication Data
Lyndsey, Anna.
    Girl in the dark : a memoir / Anna Lyndsey.
        pages   cm
        ISBN 978-0-385-53960-9 (hardcover)—
        ISBN 978-0-385-53961-6 (eBook)
    1. Lyndsey, Anna—Health. 2. Photosensitivity disorders—
Patients—England—Biography. 3. Skin—Inflammation—Patients—
England—Biography. I. Title.
    RL247.L96 2015
    616.5'15—dc23   2014030839

MANUFACTURED IN THE UNITED STATES OF AMERICA

10   9   8   7   6   5   4   3   2   1

First American Edition

For my visitors

Girl in the Dark

Part One

Light Gets In

It is extraordinarily difficult to black out a room.

First I line the curtains with blackout material, a heavy, plasticky fabric, strange flesh-like magnolia in colour, not actually black. But the light slips in easily, up and over the gap between the rail and the wall, and at the bottom through the loops made by the hanging folds.

So I add a blackout roller blind, inside the window alcove. But the light creeps in around the sides, and shimmies through the slit at the top.

So I tackle the panes themselves. I cut sheets of cooking foil, press them against the glass, tape them to the window frames. But the foil wrinkles and rips, refuses to lie flat. Gaps persist around the edges, pinpricks and tears across the middle. I tape and tape, tape over tape, foil over foil, layer upon layer. Instead of neat sheets of foil tethered by single strips of tape, the thing is becoming wild installation art. But I can't stop. The light is *laughing* at me; it is playing deliberate games, lying low to persuade me that I have made an area secure, then as soon as I move on, wriggling through some overlooked wormhole. The day beyond my window is an ocean, pressing and pulsing at my protecting walls, and I must plug a leaky dike perpetually against its power.

At last, I think I may have done enough. I lower the blind on my crazy patchwork of foil, pull the curtains, place a rolled-up towel along the crack at the bottom of the door. I sit quietly on the bed, and wait for my eyes to adjust.

And I have it. Finally I have it. I have blackness.

I lie back inside my box of darkness, the new container for my life. I am overwhelmed with exhaustion and relief.

House

The house with the blacked-out room is not a large one. It is red brick with a tiled roof, a neat 1980s box. Downstairs there is a hall, a loo, a living room and a kitchen, upstairs three modest bedrooms and a bathroom. The garage joins it to the house next door, its mirror image, round the other way.

From the front garden, looking up, my black room is the one on the right-hand side. The house, alone among its companions, has one closed eye, and inside that dark eyeball, a pale girl.

When I come out of my black room, three closed doors lead from the landing; they are always kept shut.

The stairs curve downwards into gloom, because there is a curtain covering the glazed front door. I have learnt not to hurtle down them. I descend carefully, holding on to the handrail, placing a foot squarely on each step.

I go into the living room. At each end, the curtains are drawn; they are conventional curtains, so the room is not absolutely black. Armchairs and a sofa make humped shapes like resting elephants in the minimal light. The metal frames of pictures reflect odd gleams, the images themselves invisible. Around the dining table, chair backs and arms are a jumble of vertical and horizontal bars. From a corner, a standard lamp rears a sinister outsize head.

I move into the kitchen, and immediately pick up speed. Even though closed Venetian blinds filter the light that comes through its windows, this room is much brighter than the rest of the house. I grab the kettle, shove it under the tap, slot it on to its base and bang the button down. I swing round to a cupboard, extract a mug and a plate, and sidestep to another for a teabag. I take the plate, a knife and a packet of oatcakes into the gloom next door, set them on the dining table and listen as the kettle bubbles itself to a climax. When it's clicked, I dart into the kitchen again, and with the economy and swiftness of a dancer, pour my tea, extract cheese from the fridge and, carrying both, withdraw.

Then, at the shadowy dining table, swift and concentrated eating.

For I know I do not have much time. Immediately I leave my blacked-out room, a clock is ticking; my skin begins its twisted dialogue with light. At first the exchange takes place in softest whispers, then more insistent mutterings. "Ignore it!" I want to scream. "You don't have to respond, don't get involved." But my skin soon chatters loudly, an argument is building. The situation is becoming heated; it is prudent to separate the protagonists. There are no blisters and no blotches—I am free of visible signs of conflict. But agonisingly, with ever-increasing ferocity, over the whole covering of my body, I burn with invisible fire.

I take my skin back to my lair. In the darkness, it regains its equilibrium.

Medical

... The patient now reacts not only on the uncovered areas, but even through clothing, ... resulting in severe painful reactions occurring on all areas of the body ...

DIAGNOSIS:
The working diagnosis is photosensitive seborrhoeic dermatitis. This condition certainly can cause these types of very severe reaction, these being a well-recognised though rare syndrome, which is very frequently extremely disabling as in this case because of the need to avoid even low levels of exposure to relevant light sources ...

CURRENT FUNCTIONAL CAPACITY:
This lady's light sensitivity is so severe and she is so sensitive to it (as is the case with a small group of patients whom we see with the same condition) that she is severely

incapacitated because of the extent to which she has to avoid all the various sources of light, which of course are ubiquitous in any normal environment . . . In fact, during 2006 things have been so bad that for a prolonged period of many months now she has been confined to a darkened room at home and is not able to tolerate any other situation because of her skin problem . . .

LIKELY PROGNOSIS:
Going on the experience with our other patients and on the literature about patients with these types of immediate reactions to light sources, the prognosis is very variable, but there certainly is a significant sub-set of patients whose problems persist in the long-term, sometimes very severely . . .

Talking Books

My ears become my conduit to the world. In the darkness I listen—to thrillers, to detective novels, to romances; to family sagas, potboilers and historical novels; to ghost stories and classic fiction and chick lit; to bonkbusters and history books. I listen to good books and bad books, great books and terrible books; I do not discriminate. Steadily, hour after hour, in the darkness I consume them all.

The books I listen to are random; they depend entirely on what is in the library when my book collector is there. I note down the titles on a list, divided alphabetically, so that my book collector does not bring me books I have had before. That apart, my rate of consumption is so rapid and my need so intense that I cannot afford to be fussy. There are only two curiously contrasting prohibitions on the list: "Nothing by James Patterson or Miss Read." I can live without the former's detailed descriptions of the minutiae of serial killing; the latter's accounts of the life of a village schoolmistress achieve a mixture of cattiness and smugness that render me simultaneously irritated and comatose.

For the rest, I let my authors take me where they will.

In my life before, I read at speed, skimming over the page, extracting a broad impression, seeking out salient points with a sceptical, summarising eye. Sometimes I (whisper it) *skipped descriptive passages altogether.* Now I am a captive audience and must ingest every single word. I lie back and let the plot build round me slowly, brick by brick. I collaborate willingly in my own slow seduction, for what do I want from my authors but long, long-lasting release? I come to hate interruptions in the narrative, to dread the voice which says, "That is the end of this side. The story continues on the next cassette." I grab for the next tape, scrabble it out of the tight-fitting plastic surround with my fingernails, slam it into the machine and push the button down. I am a patient on morphine whose fix has been interrupted, desperate to restart the pain-dulling feed. Close up the gaps, hurry through the changes: in those small silences despair, I know, can easily come crashing back.

By way of this unprecedented, unbridled literary promiscuity, I have made some pleasant discoveries.

Having zero interest in racing, I would never, in the life before, have picked up one of Dick Francis's horsey thrillers. But as companions in the dark, I find them amiably gripping. In one of them, the hero, a jockey-turned-accountant, is kidnapped and held in the dark in the back of a van for days, with only some bottled water and a bag of processed cheese for company; as my situation is somewhat better than his, I find this vaguely encouraging. The books celebrate the bloody-mindedness of the ordinary man: the hero will keep worrying away at a problem, and although he will certainly be knocked on the head, get tied up and suffer unpleasant consequences, he is never actually killed.

In the dark, although I listen to both, I prefer tapes to CDs. I am less likely to press the wrong button and become lost among the tracks, accidentally skipping forwards or entering a different mode, so that the sections unfurl in random order, or one repeats itself on an endless loop. In order to reverse what I have done, I have to carry my boombox downstairs, and peer at the tiny display as I poke away in the gloom.

I get to know the voices that speak to me from the corner of my dark room. There is the tough, macho chap with slightly Estuary vowels, who reads a lot of action thrillers. There is the deep-toned, chocolate-smooth voice, whose male characters are dashing and manly, but whose females, rendered in falsetto, all sound faintly imbecilic. There is the elegiac, lugubrious Michael Jayston, who specialises in the world-weary melancholy of P. D. James and John le Carré, and Miriam Margolyes, who creates so many characters with such distinctive voices that it is difficult to believe that there is only one woman in there, and not a troupe.

When I finish a book, I find I cannot start another one immediately. Each book needs time to settle in my mind, to be digested like a meal of many courses. It seems disrespectful to the characters to move on too quickly—after all, I have spent hours in their company, learnt their histories, looked on at significant moments of their lives. I still have nagging questions echoing in my mind: surely someone would have noticed the substitution of the bodies? Why in American crime fiction do people eat so much pizza?

During these intermissions, I put on Radio 4. It can be counted on to provide an unceasing stream of trivial earnestness, a gentle showerbath for the soul.

Moving About

When I am first in the dark, I frequently get lost. Even though the room is only a small space filled with simple objects—a bed, a bookshelf, a wardrobe, a bureau—the darkness can cause disorientation that is total, and terrifying. In my early days I find myself patting my hands across surfaces I cannot identify, feeling frantically for some sort of clue. Often my mind is absolutely convinced I am sitting on the floor facing in one direction, and then my hands start telling me something else. I cry out. The cognitive dissonance is overwhelming, like a physical rending of my brain.

But this rarely happens now. I am in my element.

I move confidently about my box of darkness, lay my hand easily on the cotton-covered firmness of the bed, grasp the chair in the corner by the smooth curved poles that form its back, reach for the cool metal handle of the door and hear its catlike creak.

Sometimes I lose a sock, or my hairbrush, but there is no panic now, I feel calmly in each likely place, slowly passing from one to the other, and usually the object is found.

Gradually I do what is not in my nature; I develop routines: socks always go *there*, spectacles *there*. One day I reorganise my underwear drawer so that knickers are on the left and bras on the right. This puts an end to wild morning burrowing and flailing—I wonder why I have not done it before. But I know the answer to that. Simply—hope. Hope held me back. Each small accommodation of my physical environment is an admission that things are not improving, that this is not some fleeting horror, that perhaps . . .

But that is the unthinkable thought.

There is only one circumstance, now, where I can lose my orientation. Sometimes, in one of my small attempts to keep moving, to keep the blood flowing, I march on the spot. Often, I find, after a few minutes, that I have turned through 90 degrees, that the bed, rather than being beside me, is in front.

An anecdote told by a character in a thriller brings me the explanation. A man, lost in the Sahara, decides the best way out is to walk forward in a straight line. After several miles, he finds himself in the place where he started. Human legs are never of exactly equal length;

you may believe you walk straight ahead, but slowly, imperceptibly, your course will curve, you will tread a circle, and your beginning will be your end.

Pete

In the house with the drawn curtains and the sealed-up room, there is a second person living.

He is Pete, the person that I love. It is his house I wear, his rooms I have dimmed to quarter-light, his spare bedroom I have commandeered to make my lair.

My love has saved me. It wraps strong arms around me when I cry with despair; it gives me the routine of a working week to lend vicarious structure to my shapeless days. It brings me daily laughter, a reason to keep washing . . .

. . . and it slices me open with guilt. For I am creating two shadow lives, where there need only be one. I am sucking the light from Pete's life, leaving him a twilit, liminal creature, single yet not single, who at social events sits alone among the couples, with a strange absent presence always by his side.

I argue with myself during my long periods alone. I undertake lengthy ethical investigations and conduct detailed philosophical analyses. I am trying to discern the behaviour that would, in my circumstances, be morally right. Should I leave him?

This would be difficult, practically; it would require time, research and careful organisation—but it could just about be done. I would need to find another place to live, with another blacked-out room; either a place on my own, with people nearby who could be paid to do my shopping, or a place with someone who was prepared to look after me, prepared to close doors before they switch on lights, pull curtains before I come into a room; someone I could trust, because I would be at their mercy.

I pummel my conscience for an answer. By staying, by shirking the responsibility and effort of leaving, by continuing to occupy this lovely man while giving him neither children nor a public companion nor a welcoming home—do I do wrong?

This is how I reason, hour after hour. Then I hear his key in the door, and his tread on the stairs. I hear him call out "Wotcher, chuck!" and stomp about in the bedroom next door as he takes off his shoes and tie and puts on his slippers. Then he knocks at my door, and I say "Come in," and scramble up to hug him.

And all my ethical reasoning crumbles to ash in the sheer fact of his presence. Because together, even in darkness, we light up a room; because the clotted guilt inside me breaks up and disperses before a surge of stupid happiness; because I love him, and I know I cannot leave him, am incapable of leaving him, unless he asks me to go.

And he has not asked me.

And that is the miracle which I live with, every day.

Domestic

"What's for dinner?" Pete asks, coming in to see me one Friday evening after he arrives home from work. I haven't made any dinner, but I have conceptualised it, and done something about certain of its component parts. "There's some left-over salad in a bowl in the fridge," I say, "and I defrosted some smoked salmon. So, if you could boil some potatoes?"

"Sounds manageable," says Pete, and goes off downstairs. He is not good at cooking. I try to keep his instructions simple, whilst still obtaining for us both a diet that is reasonably varied and healthy.

"OKAY!" Pete roars from below when the meal is ready. He's turned off the main lights in the living room, and switched on a little lamp with a 25-watt bulb, which sits behind the TV cabinet. It is at one end of the room, and the dining table is at the other, so we can just about see each other, and what we are eating.

"So how have things been today?" he asks. (Sometimes even my brief forays out of the darkness reignite me, and the burning can take days to subside. Very occasionally, I have had to be fed in my room, on a tray.)

"Oh, much as usual," I reply. "I'm listening to this bonkers talking book at the moment, about this group of friends training to be international bankers, and one of them is a psychopath. It's kind of obvious who the psychopath is, but the characters take for ever to figure it out. Anyway, I got fed up and stopped listening for a bit and I heard this great programme on the radio. A bloke was in India trying to record the roar of the Bengal tiger, and when he got one it sounded incredible, really deep and resonant, sort of like . . ."

I attempt to roar like a Bengal tiger.

"Yes, thank you, darling, it's just like being there."

"Well, you know, in broad terms . . . I haven't really got the chest expansion. He also said that tigers are very territorial and like to patrol, so they can often be seen walking along roads in the national park."

"Actually, I've seen a few pictures at the camera club of tigers walking along roads. One guy is going to India next month to photograph them. He'll be stuck in a hide for hours, five nights in a row, but he's always sitting in bushes waiting for birds, so presumably he's used to it."

Pete is not into wildlife photography. He prefers taking pictures of landscapes, and, in particular, of trees.

I ask, "How was work?"

"I did some calculations this morning," says Pete, "and then the mainframe went down, so that was the end of that. Then Morose Man came to see me. He was even less talkative than usual. And I had a meeting with Bulgy-eyed Boss."

"Oh goodness. Did he bulge at you?"

"Not at me, this time. But he did a classic on Corporate Man. He said, 'I'm looking to YOU,' and bulged at him over the top of his spectacles."

"Scary stuff."

"It was. Do you want any afters?"

"I'd like some fruit, please. There should be grapes in the fridge."

Once we've finished eating, I retreat to my lair, and he does the washing-up.

At eight o'clock I switch on *Any Questions* and Pete joins me in the dark. After a hard week at the office, he likes to relax by listening to political types lay into each other on Radio 4. *Any Questions* is not my favourite programme, but this is one thing we can do together. I lie beside him on the narrow bed, exclaiming at intervals:

"They've completely missed the point!"

"This is just a load of platitudes."

"Is this idiot still talking? I'll put my head under the pillow, and you can nudge me when he's finished."

"Try not to get so worked up, darling," says Pete, holding me. "We're only on question one."

Thus passes our Friday night.

Dreams

Oh, what can I not do, in my dreams.

In my dreams I travel on trains and climb mountains, I play concerts and swim rivers, I carry important documents on vital missions, I attend meetings which become song-and-dance routines. My body lies boxed in darkness, but beneath my closed eyelids there is colour, sound and movement, in glorious contrast to the day; mad movies projected nightly in the private theatre of my skull.

My dreams are crowded with people, as though to compensate for the solitariness of my waking hours. People I know, famous people, people from obscure parts of my past whom I thought I had forgotten, people I don't know at all, spontaneously generated in some crevice of my brain, people who are disturbing incarnations of my deepest hopes and fears. People come together in strange, mixed-up groups—my aunt and John Humphrys, a girl I was at school with, a former colleague; bizarre in retrospect, but at the time having the compelling logic of dreams.

To wake is always horrible, plunging suddenly down a long dark chute to thump gracelessly on to the mattress. "Stop, stop," I cry to the escaping dream, "I want you still." But the dream speeds away to the horizon, and I am left clutching only a few remembered fragments, strands plucked from the vanishing tail.

Animals in zoos and prisoners sleep many hours a day. Like them I have become a devotee, a voluptuary of sleep, a connoisseur of its intense, uncharted pleasures. Sleep slips the chains of this life, snaps the intimate fetters of my skin, sets me free to travel the wild landscapes of the ungoverned mind. Each night I enter by the same door, yet find behind it something new. I plunge my hands into the lucky dip of dreams; sometimes I find sweets, and sometimes scorpions, but always, for a few hours, deliverance.

Dream 1

I am on a train just outside Waterloo Station. It is packed with commuters—I am lucky to have got a window seat. I look out over the ridges and furrows of railway tracks, bunching into a thick brown swathe as they approach the terminus. Through the gaps between office buildings, I glimpse the silver skeleton of the London Eye.

I am dreaming my journey to work. When the train pulls into platform 2, I am swept out of the carriage and over the concourse by a surge of dark suits. Everyone seems purposeful and determined, carrying briefcases and bags, and walking in the same direction. I am borne down the steps into York Road, under the railway, and up on to Hungerford Bridge.

The panorama of London opens out around me—the Southbank Centre behind and to my right, the Houses of Parliament upstream on the opposite bank, Embankment Gardens, Charing Cross Station, the Savoy Hotel. The huge grey Thames, plunging through the centre of the city, creates a glorious canyon of light, distance and rushing air, an antidote to boxy offices and car-packed streets.

In my dream the sky above me is full of bustling white clouds, and the river beneath me seethes with porpoises and whales, rolling and basking, and suddenly surfacing, so that water pours down their smooth grey sides.

I speed over the bridge, full of confidence and hope. I know I've been away from work, but I'm sure I'm better now. I enter my office through huge gold-coloured doors which swing open at my approach. But my colleagues appear to be the same. "Glad to see you back," they say. "There's a lot on at the moment. The Minister needs a briefing paper by ten o'clock. We've set you up in a desk in the corner, so you can keep the overhead lights switched off."

"That's sensible," I think. I go to my desk, settle into my chair and turn on my machine.

But I can't make it work. Things come up on the screen that I didn't type in at the keyboard. Files and applications open and close randomly. The mouse is recalcitrant under my hand, while the cursor zips round the screen. Thousands of emails pour down upon me.

I wake up in a panic. "I must get that computer sorted out," I think. "But at least I got to work. That was pretty good." Then I open my eyes into darkness, and realise that I have gone nowhere, and remember that I am not even in London any more.

And I think back to the life I had before, a life of very ordinary components, with the usual balance of frustration and contentment, the standard complement of light and shade. And I remember the beginnings of the darkness, and where it planted its first roots, smack into the centre of that life.

April 2005

I am at my computer, typing hard. Around me banks of desks stretch out, studded with hunched bodies. The ends of rows are marked with lurid rose-pink filing cabinets, a strange attempt by management to make the new high-density seating arrangement seem vibrant and fun.

Fingers tap on keyboards, mouths mutter into

phones, printers burp and heave. The low ceiling presses down on us, pocked with fluorescent squares. People cross the space from time to time, to discuss things discreetly with colleagues. An intriguing lone declaration breaks periodically from the well-modulated hum:

"Tell Press Office that's all we can say."

Or "Hey, where's Chris this afternoon?"

Or "Bloody HR are driving me mad."

It is the headquarters of the Department of Work and Pensions, a week before the general election in 2005.

Everyone expects Labour to win, though with a reduced majority. Tony Blair will take the opportunity to reshuffle his team, and we will get yet another Minister for Pensions, who will have to be got up to speed. I am writing a paper for this unknown politician, currently on the campaign trail in Glasgow, or Bolton, or Northampton, festooned with balloons and red rosettes, and answering awkward questions about the war in Iraq.

Lucid paragraphs flow on to my screen. I know what the Minister needs to know, and how to explain the complicated bits so that even an idiot will understand. Facts and arguments are easily accessible, neatly marshalled inside my head.

And inside another part of my head: chaos, panic and terror.

On and on. Round and round. Thoughts writhing beneath my calm, professional exterior like a basement of black snakes. *I cannot lose my job. I don't know how much longer I can go on like this. I have to keep going. How can I keep going? I cannot lose my job.*

I love my job—it is at times bizarre, frustrating and

surreal, but always interesting: the curious compound language of cricketing metaphor and management jargon, the strange parliamentary procedures, the politicians' egos, the old, old certainties of power.

And I love its location—just a little way east of the stone desolation of Whitehall, which we nonetheless visit frequently, to see our ministers, or the suave types at the Treasury, or en route to the Palace of Westminster itself. In my lunch break I can walk easily to Covent Garden, where I mooch zombie-like among the clothes shops, filling my eyes with colour and pattern to blot out the strains of the day. At a tiny takeaway run by two Italians, I find my favourite office lunch—a baked potato with tuna and black olive pâté, in generous, gleaming scoops. Even closer is Embankment Gardens, a slender tongue of city nature, where, under pressure to unknot some problem by some ridiculous deadline, I wander among the bright flowerbeds and the big mature trees, and gain new insight and perspective.

My parents, both professional musicians, were precariously self-employed, and my childhood was punctuated by periodic crises when my father would announce dramatically that the orchestra (he was a cellist with the London Philharmonic) was about to go under, and we were all going to end up in the workhouse. It never quite happened—the orchestra teetered on from one savage grant reduction to the next—but perhaps the whole experience had a psychological effect, predisposing me to join the civil service in search of boring job security and defined benefit pensions.

I have just bought a flat, after years of false starts and

deals falling through (roof repairs, psychopathic neighbours, asbestos, leases that couldn't be extended—the usual stuff experienced by people trying to buy non-modern one-bedroom flats in unposh parts of south London). Now, at last, all the weird things I've accumulated over the years, without having anywhere to put them—a gold sunburst clock, a leopard-print teapot, vintage curtains, an upright piano—are coming out of boxes and cupboards and the spare room at my mother's, and finding their proper place. All my pent-up interior design projects are bursting forth—I've always wanted a yellow-painted kitchen, and a wall full of arty postcards, and a big curly iron bed.

So I cannot lose my job. I cannot lose my job. I cannot lose this flat, this longed-for realisation of my dream.

At first, it happened only occasionally. I had the odd bad day, then things reverted to normal. Gradually, the bad days became more frequent, they oozed into each other, they coalesced. The good days became the exceptions, small islands of diminishing hope.

Now even the islands have gone.

So what is it, this strange, unprecedented thing? Simply this: when I sit in front of a computer screen, the skin on my face burns.

Burns?

Burns like the worst kind of sunburn. Burns like someone is holding a flame-thrower to my head.

To the left of my computer is my desperate short-term solution: a small electric fan, propped on a directory, angled to blow air continuously across my face. As soon as I shift away from the airstream, the pain comes thumping back.

I've been to the doctor's and explained the problem. The GP, puzzled and concerned, has put me on a waiting list to see a dermatologist. Perhaps, in the interim, I should take sick leave—but I am possessed by a strange delusion of indispensability. I honestly believe that if I were not here, this important paper about pensions would not be written so well; the new Minister, robbed of my lucid expertise, would fail to grasp the issues; decisions would not be taken, implementation dates would slip.

I don't want to let down my team. And I do not wish even to consider the possibility that the mysterious process afoot in my flesh could ultimately divide me from the job I love—the job which has formed me over the past ten years, which pays for all the structures of my life.

If for one millisecond the veil of the future could be raised, and I could catch one glimpse of the terrifying tunnel ahead, I would be immune to any claims of conscience, any sense of loyalty, any of the contumely heaped upon shirkers. I would run from that office, down John Adam Street, up the steps of Hungerford Bridge, over the river to where the homeless people live, as if a fiend pursued me; I would abandon at one stroke my job, my mortgage and my comfortable life, and I would stay with them, sleeping on cardboard and swaddled in blankets, but still possessed of the freedom of the city, and with the sky above my head.

But I do not know my future, and am sensible only of the pressures of the present. So I stay at my post, typing fiercely, the fan feebly cooling my face.

May 2005

"Welcome," says the Chair of the meeting, an avuncular type with large black-framed spectacles and a balding head. He is known for his humane and relaxed approach, which he is going to need, because this is a meeting at which thirty line managers attempt to rank staff in order of performance, for the purposes of end-of-year reports.

The meeting is taking place in a subterranean, windowless room, with off-white fibreboard walls, a dirty grey carpet and ferocious fluorescent lights. Grey tables are set out round the edges, in the form of a hollow square. People are tanking up on sour-smelling coffee, and looking round suspiciously at their colleagues. I am, unusually, pleased to be here, because it means several hours away from my computer, during which my face will have some respite. Although someone has deliberately chosen a particularly horrible room, presumably to encourage us to reach consensus, it is not going to happen quickly.

"But does he really go the extra mile? I've come across him in meetings, and I have to say he lacks sparkle."

"And if you compare him with Anthony, who's really shone this year . . ."

"Actually, my team have had a lot of problems dealing with Anthony. It seems impossible to get him to co-operate in any way. And he's always out at lunch."

"Surely the key deciding factor should be: does he live the Departmental values?"

"Oh, for God's sake, that's not going to get us anywhere."

"Well, what do you suggest?"

It is a hopeless task. The staff under consideration, although all of the same grade, do wildly different jobs in different parts of the department. Some are known to other line managers and some are unknown, while others have been glimpsed across a crowded meeting room or encountered in the pub, and entirely subjective judgements have been formed. Some managers prove to be cunning and devious advocates, others are far too honest, and easily put on the defensive.

Truly, it is the meeting from hell. After three hours I am still trying to follow the discussion and intervene where it would help my staff. But something strange is happening which is claiming more and more of my attention. There are no screens in this fiercely lit, sub-terranean box, yet my face is on fire, nonetheless. I find myself sitting forward, elbows on the table, hands pressed to my cheeks, trying to give my face protection, or at least the comfort of touch. There are bottles of water dotted around, and I pour myself glass after glass.

Finally the squabbles are over. Compromises have been made, or people have just given up. The air in the room is rank with coffee, sweat and acrimony. "Thank you very much, everybody," says the Chair, and I rush for the door. My colleague Tina is beside me, saying, "Blimey, that was grim." But I am not in a state to reply.

I leave the office and catch the train home. When I get there, I collapse on my bed. My mind is a careful and complete blank—for the time being, I've given up trying to seek explanations or make connections. I'm just overwhelmed by the reality of pain.

I don't have to wait long. Over the next few days, the answer forces its pattern into my consciousness, like the words of a brand: my face now reacts to fluorescent lights as well.

I'm starting to see that I can't carry on. Two trains of thought have been running on parallel tracks in my mind, speeding towards a single set of points: I am in agony, I must keep going.

There is going to be a smash.

AT THREE O'CLOCK in the afternoon, I go to see my boss. I tell him that the pain is now unbearable, that I need to go home, take some time off. In any case, I'm due to go on leave next week. My boss is very sympathetic. "Don't worry, we'll cope," he says. "Now you go and get yourself better." I switch off my computer, sling my bag over my shoulder and walk across the big murmuring room. In the foyer, I pass the security guard and push through the swing doors at the front of the building, coming out on to John Adam Street, voluptuously empty under a brilliant late May sky. I breathe in the intoxicating smell of summer in the city—warm tarmac and baked refuse, mixed with something floral and vibrant, as if the air itself were blossoming. Just the smell is usually enough to make my spirits lift, my mind tingle with possibilities. Today, I pass through the glory of the afternoon like a walking corpse.

Halfway towards Villiers Street, I glance down at my hand and notice with a start that I am still holding my office mug, and that it is half-full of tea. It is a cheerful green mug with a silly cartoon, a present from my former team when I moved to my current job. I stop and stare dazedly at it, not knowing what to do. Then, down in the gutter, I spy a metal drain. I pour the tea away between its elongated fangs, shaking out the final drips before stowing it in my bag.

The body has an unconscious wisdom that the mind denies. My hand, holding the mug, grasps the truth that I will not be back, but I still cling to hope.

June 2005

I am on a boat, slipping between white sky and silky grey sea. It is late morning in early June, and the high sun is intense behind the taut dome of haze. Leaning my elbows on the wooden rail, letting the wind blow on my face, I look out to the first of the Farne Islands, a weird black squiggle afloat on the North Sea.

I turn my head and smile as I see Pete, camera to his face, taking a photo of me and the island. I'm wearing a straw hat tied tightly round the crown with a bright scarf to stop it from blowing away. Having very pale skin and an undertone of red in my dark brown hair, I've always sheltered under wide brims while others went bareheaded or sported tiny baseball caps. As a student, on a conservation work camp in Germany one summer, I was such a curiosity that I was photographed for the local paper—an eccentric Englishwoman in an enormous hat.

Pete and I are on holiday in Northumberland. I was unsure, at this crisis of my life, whether to go or not, but everyone agreed it would be a good thing to get out of London. "The great outdoors, fresh air, time to chill out, de-stress—you'll soon be feeling better."

Ah stress, that great explanatory factor. And indeed, I am starting to relax, on this small, gleaming, tourist-heavy boat, as it ploughs away from the Northumberland coast towards these unknown rough-hewn islands, strange citadels of birds. The tension slides off my shoulders like a stiff uncomfortable coat and the writhing knot of panic in my mind comes to rest, the snakes gently untangling themselves and wriggling away. Under the influence of emptiness, of vastness, my mind empties too, and finds, if not peace, at least a sort of truce.

The boat arrives at the main island, bumping up against a jetty beside a small beach. There is a visitor centre here and a wooden slatted path to follow, in order to observe the different colonies of birds.

"The first birds you'll come to are the Arctic terns," says the boatman. "It's the nesting season, so they can be aggressive."

We are already among them as we crunch across the beach; they squeak and skitter around our ankles, with their white undersides ending in sharply forked tails, grey wings, blood-red bills and neat black skullcaps pulled down over their eyes.

"In what way are they aggressive?" I ask Pete, as we turn up a slatted walkway between lush hummocks of grass peppered with nesting terns.

"Oh, they dive-bomb you," he answers nonchalantly. "Don't worry about it. It happened to me in Iceland."

At that moment I feel a sharp thump on the side of my head and the flurry of wings as the tern swoops away. Then there is another impact and another. I raise my arms to try to protect my face. It is not, by any means, pain-free, and I am glad I am wearing my hat, because those blood-red beaks could certainly draw blood.

Pete, having wandered on up the path, has turned round to photograph the action. No terns, I notice, are attacking him. I lower my head and hurry forwards, receiving farewell stabs on the back and scalp. I am feeling extremely cross and put out, having observed before that Pete has a reassuring and calming effect on animals, while I always seem to upset them. On our many country walks, berserk dogs will gambol playfully about him, before holding me at bay against a tree.

But then I remember that when I first met Pete, he had a calming and reassuring effect on me as well. I was sitting hopelessly on a sofa in a hotel in Devon, on the first evening of a group walking holiday, wishing I had not come. I had just been trying to make conversation with a couple of insipid secretaries, and was sure they thought I was a weirdo. Everyone else had gone through to dinner, and I stared wearily at the flowers on the carpet, asking myself why I had ever thought a holiday alone with a bunch of strangers might conceivably be a good idea.

"So—where have you come from?"

I looked up, and saw a man standing in the doorway, facing back into the room. I noticed that he was long and thin, and stooped forward slightly to address me, in a friendly way.

"I'm from Wimbledon," I said. "South-west London."

"Ah," he replied. "Where the tennis is."

Slowly, I got up from my sofa and walked across to him. "Well, I say Wimbledon," I said, smiling, "because people have heard of it, but I don't actually live in the posh bit. What about you?"

"I'm from Itchingford. It's a town in Hampshire—more towards the south than the north."

"Hmm. Interesting place name. I hope it's not descriptive."

"Oh, Hampshire is full of silly names. There's Popham and Lasham and Cosham and, of course, Nether Wallop."

"Goodness," I said. "It all sounds very violent."

We entered the large dining room, where about fifty people sat around long tables and the noise of talk bounced off the walls, and he took me to join the friends he had come with, who seemed to be nice, and the dinner was tasty, and everything began to look more cheerful.

The holiday in Devon lasted a week and, as is the way of these things, I spent the first five days lusting after someone else. He was a loud, posh, super-confident person called Marcus, a natural social leader, quite unlike myself. He had pale, translucent skin, black-brown hair and a very square head which seemed as though it ought to have a bolt through it. The only time I spoke to him alone, after he'd helped me over a stile, we managed to antagonise each other within minutes. He made some crack about the boringness of civil servants, and I gave an unnecessarily savage response.

Oh, but I watched him from afar. I was constantly aware of him, I could have told you, at every point of every day, where he was and what he was doing (easier with him than with another person, actually, because of the loudness of his voice). Such is the hopeless obtuseness of lust.

On the penultimate day we went to Dartmoor for our walk. Everything was shrouded in thick grey fog that oozed soft droplets on to our coats and faces, and made it impossible to see more than a hundred metres in any direction. But the air was mild and sweet, full of herby moorland flavours.

I trudged up a long gentle rise covered in tufted yellow grass towards a tor at the top, a mad sculpture of massive grey boulders piled on one another in contiguous columns like a collapsed abacus. Kathy, a placid blonde woman, one of Pete's group of friends, was walking with me, chatting. Suddenly, she said, apropos of nothing, "So what do you think of Pete?"

"Well . . ." I said, rather taken aback, "he seems a bit lugubrious—but nice, definitely nice."

Kathy smiled and went on, "He's taken rather a sh—"

and then abruptly broke off and began talking about the weather. But I wasn't listening, because I had heard the words she didn't say, as clearly as if she'd shouted them into my ear—"shine to you, he's taken rather a shine to you"—and an explosion had gone off in my head.

The others were already at the top and there were only a few metres of yellow grass in which to compose myself before I was there too. Weird glittering fragments were still flying round my skull, as though a lens through which I'd seen the world had disintegrated beneath a laser's beam. Why waste time on Frankenstein's monster, I asked myself, who is clearly arrogant, unpleasant and unobtainable, when there is this other chap who you actually like talking to, and who looks not uninteresting—in fact, who resembles a craggy blond vampire, complete with deadpan humour and slightly pointy teeth.

It was unfortunate that I had realised this just as the holiday was about to end.

I scrambled up an angled slab of rock and stood gingerly upright on top of the tor, staring at the panoramic non-view. A faint patchwork of browns, purples and greens lay under the fog, like a filthy old quilt in an attic, covered in cobwebs and dust. I was alone on an island in a sinister grey sea that floated upwards all around me to merge with the sky. Uncertainly, I shifted my feet on my narrow perch, suddenly aware that it was slippery, and that I was not sure how to descend. I noticed Pete standing on the ground beside my boulder, looking upwards, a blond head against the grey. "Would you like a hand down?" he asked gravely, stretching out an arm. I placed my hand in his, and jumped.

Now, having got together, split up and got together again, we have been reunited for two years, and have made it past the violent terns on to the highest part of this low-slung, treeless island. "We're lucky they weren't Arctic skuas," says Pete.

"Why, what do they do?" I ask.

"Oh, they're very fierce. They pursue you well away from their nesting sites, and then they sku-a you."

To this sort of thing, a groan is the only possible response.

The slatted walkway meets another going across at right angles, and in one of the corners made by the joining of the paths, there is what appears at first to be a heap of earth and stones. Struck by some oddity of texture, I look again—and realise that the muddy heap has two brown eyes and a long brown beak, and that it is actually a female eider duck, its feathers comfortably fluffed out, perfectly camouflaged against the ground. "One can see why it would make a good duvet," I say, as we stand on the walkway admiring it. The duck sits on, presumably hatching something, pillowy and unperturbed.

On the rest of our walk, we see puffins popping in and out of puffin burrows scraped into the flat featureless turf, an unexpectedly prosaic setting for such an arty-looking bird. We stand at the top of an inlet, its sheer sides drenched in guano, and inhale the mixed stench of salt, shit and fish as we look down on colonies of kittiwakes and auks. The latter look like corporate types attending a formal event, with their smart black plumage, white shirt fronts and tendency to stand about in rows on outsize patent-leather feet.

Back on the boat, we cruise around the other islands, but do not land. These are the private bailiwicks of birds, birds in their thousands, birds stacked on shelves of black rock, perched in jostling rows on top of low cliffs, bouncing across expanses of turf, shrieking, rasping, swooping, diving, living their intense unfathomable lives.

I say to Pete, "I can see why people get obsessed by birds. They're probably the wild creature that most people see most often, and in greatest profusion."

"Yes," he replies. "Or at least in parts of the world where herds of wildebeest are less common. And there are lots of different sorts, so you get to check them off a list, which people really like."

"If I were a bird," I say dreamily, "I think I'd be a gannet. I would get to do those amazing dives, from hundreds of feet in the air, head first into the sea. I remember watching them when I was small, on holiday on the Isle of Arran, with my mum and dad."

Pete laughs and puts his arm round me. "Head for heights, voracious appetite, likes fish," he says. "Sounds appropriate."

"How rude," I retort. "Anyway, how about you?"

He looks into the distance, considering. "I think I'd be an owl," he says judiciously, and suddenly I'm overwhelmed with love for him, as though those six short words have released some warm bright substance into my system, and it is surging through my veins.

We huddle together on the hard narrow seats that line the deck of the boat. Three hours have passed since the start of the trip, and the sky is growing greyer. The small amount of colour that the islands possess drains away and the seascape becomes a study in monochrome. A chilly wind has sprung up and the boat plunges and soars as it noses its way through the swell. Leaving the last of the islands, it begins a wide arc towards home.

The change in direction means a shift in our position relative to the wind. The current of air which has been blowing past me ceases, and I become aware of something that up to now I have failed to notice, or perhaps that I have been refusing to notice, have kept pushing back below the surface of consciousness like an inconveniently buoyant corpse.

My face.

My face.

The tension that fell from me earlier in the day rears up from the deck of the boat. It binds itself round my body, tighter and fiercer than before.

I have followed everyone's advice. I am here in the wildness, in the emptiness, surrounded only by elemental things: sea and air and rock and sky. I have removed myself from the artificial environment of the office, fetid with the stench of deadlines and the plasticky fumes of computers. There are no fluorescent lights or screens. There is only—

There is only the sun.

The human body is an amazing thing. Parts of it

gamely keep functioning, even as other parts reel. My hands grip the edges of the wooden bench and my heart zigzags inside my chest. My vision is blurring and I can hardly get air into my lungs. But my voice remains calm. I hear myself chatting to Pete about birds, and what we might do for dinner, and the shots he wants to take of Dunstanburgh Castle, and our rather ghastly room at the B&B, all dark MDF and glass ornaments with a view into a hedge and the base of a telegraph pole. I listen to our laughter as though from outside of myself, and am astonished at how normal I sound.

I do not want to spoil this day, this lovely day of birds and sky. I want to keep it whole and pure so I can hold it in my mind, a talisman against whatever is to come.

It is only in the evening, back in our weird B&B, that, my face on fire, I let go and howl. Pete holds me in his arms on the cramped double bed. "Oh God, this is the end," I cry. "It's got to be the sunlight. It can't be anything else."

Neither of us knows what to do. We pass a sleepless night, rigid, side by side, a pair of waxworks under the slippery purple quilt.

The next day, I decide to go home. I leave Pete to have the rest of the holiday, to visit Dunstanburgh and Lindisfarne, and take photographs in the pure light of midsummer in this land of vast beaches and infinite sky. At Alnmouth, he puts me on to an intercity train. It is hard to know what we mean when we say goodbye. "Wish me luck," I say.

"Good luck," he replies.

And I flee from the ironic and agonising beauty,

bolting like an animal to its lair. Something is afoot within me that I do not understand, the breaking of a contract that I thought could not be broken, a slow perverting of my very substance.

June 2005—Later

Pete comes to see me in London after the holiday. I am in a state, my face now definitely reacting to light. But the sensitivity seems to change at random, making it hard to establish how much I can tolerate, and how bright. Sometimes the curtains need to stay shut, sometimes it is OK to go for a walk towards evening, occasionally I make it to the shops, at other times any of these activities causes horrible burning that lasts for hours. So many places, I am discovering, have fluorescent lighting—buses, trains, supermarkets, the GP's surgery, which I visit to be signed off work. I have taken to wearing my straw hat and a long cotton scarf round my neck that I can hold up over the lower part of my face. It mitigates, but does not remove, the pain of exposure.

I know that it would be good for me to leave smelly London, and stop trying to cope on my own. I do not know what is happening to my relationship with Pete; most likely it is crumbling—everything else in my life seems to be coming to an end. But I haven't got time for niceties and subtleties, the way one is supposed to negotiate with a boyfriend of two years. A ferocious drive for self-preservation has grown up within me, and it has eaten most of my pride.

We sit in the small kitchen at the back of my first-floor flat. Cool drinks stand on the pine table, and outside summer rages, in a riot of dayglo blue and green.

I take his hand across the corner of the table. There is one particular possibility that I have to eliminate or confirm. "I'm going to ask you something," I say, "and please don't worry about saying no. I will absolutely understand."

"OK," he says. "What is it?"

The words wait behind my lips, I feel them push against my teeth. How strange, I think, suddenly detached, that mere vibrations released into air can change the course of lives.

I take a breath and let the words fly free. "Can I come and stay with you for a while?" I look past his head, at the kitchen shelves with their piles of plates and bowls. "I'm sorry to have to ask."

He says nothing. For I am asking, of course, for more than house room. I am asking him to help me interact with the outside world, and to burden himself with a girlfriend who is rapidly becoming a freak.

"Can I think about it?" he says.

"Of course you can." I squeeze his hand. "Now, what shall we do about dinner?" I get up from the table, and find my legs are shaking and can hardly bear my weight.

Later that night, I can't sleep. I turn over in my mind what the other options might be if he says no, focusing on ruthlessly practical thoughts. I try to anaesthetise myself to the true implications of what I have done—

that if he says no, it means that everything is over, and I face the future alone.

We make inconsequential small talk over breakfast. I try to divine from his manner what is going on in his mind, but what words lurk behind his lips I cannot tell.

Eventually he says, "I've thought about what you asked. I must say I didn't sleep much last night. Anyway, I've decided yes."

Relief crashes over me in a huge clean wave. "Thank you," I say, jumping up to hug him.

"I think we should have a trial period," he continues, "just to see how it goes. Say two months?"

In my guts, I feel a clutch of dismay. So then—not completely overwhelmed with delight. But I should have expected something of this sort. Pete is organised, orderly and circumspect, in contrast to my more spontaneous nature. We complement each other—it is why things have worked well.

So I hug him again, and force away my misgivings, and say, "Yes, that's a sensible idea. Who knows? A few weeks in the same house and we might both go barking mad."

"Woof," he says, and kisses my neck.

IF WE COULD only see the future.

Reacting on my face is bad, but surely hats, scarves and avoidance will be the limit of my limitations? We have no inkling of the strange reversal that awaits us, that within a year, relieving my face will transfer the problem, intensified, to the rest of me, and immure me, helpless, in the dark.

We will look back, then, to this time as to a golden age, and if we ever could rerun this day, knowing what will come, I am quite sure he would not take me in, and as for me, I know that I would never dare to ask.

Games to Play in the Dark

Necessity is the mother of invention.

In the dark you have only the materials of voice, mind and memory, and the mind's eye, powerful or wavering depending on how you are feeling. So the games you play in the dark use words. And the words are little sparks in the darkness, because they make something flash up in your consciousness, as on a computer screen. Each one is a tiny stimulus, a mental pinprick; one of those jolts of electricity that keep you alive.

Games to Play in the Dark 1: Transformation

This is a game to play on your own, at night, when you can't sleep. It disciplines the mind, requiring the kind of concentration that excludes all other thoughts.

Think of two words with the same number of letters.

In your mind, change one into the other by changing one letter at a time. Every new combination of letters must also make a word.

Sometimes you will find you have gone up a blind alley and must retrace your steps to try a different route. Sometimes you will find you have gone round a long and complicated diversion when a short cut existed all the time.

BLACK can become WHITE. BODY can become SOUL. DEATH . . . LIVES.

BLACK	BODY	DEATH
SLACK	BODE	HEATH
SLICK	BOLE	HEATS
SLICE	BOLL	HEAPS
SPICE	BOIL	HELPS
SPINE	SOIL	HELLS
SHINE	SOUL	HALLS
SHITE		MALLS
WHITE		MALES
		SALES
		SAVES
		LAVES
		LIVES

And my tour de force, the only six-letter transformation I ever achieved. One hot, airless, enclosed summer night, I turned BUTTER into CHEESE.

BUTTER
BATTER
BATTED
BAITED
WAITED

WHITED
WHITES
WHINES
SHINES
SPINES
SPICES
SLICES
SLICKS
CLICKS
CLOCKS
CHOCKS
CHECKS
CHEEKS
CHEERS
CHEERY
CHEESY
CHEESE

Energy

In my darkness, I feel full of beans. I could run for miles across open country, dance the whole night through, turn cartwheels over sea-scrubbed sand. My brain is unfogged, my mind is clear. Life and energy crackle in my limbs, my neural networks hum.

I am the prisoner only of my skin—would I could claw that traitorous membrane from my bones.

The darkness can sense the anomaly at its core; that lump of energised matter, throbbing against the clutch of its confinement, as though a tin can contained a beating heart.

But the darkness has its own quiet wisdom. Slowly, subtly, it will moderate that futile energy; it has methods for restoring equilibrium.

Eyes close when there is nothing for them to see; it is a natural response. When eyes are closed, alertness dims, thoughts turn inward, breathing slows. The body relaxes, it questions the need to be vertical, it longs to measure its length on the bed or the floor. After all, that is where, in darkness, a body feels most secure, least likely to become disorientated, to tangle with the furniture, or bash extremities against the wall.

In my sealed-up room, the darkness whispers to my body with a thousand gentle tongues. "Rest," it says, passing soft fingers over my eyelids, pulling me downwards with insistent hands. It has a thousand gentle mouths to press against my flesh, and suck, so tenderly, my energy away.

I often succumb. It feels so easy and so natural, to give in to that wise, compassionate caress. But I know I should resist. I do not want to waste away, my muscles slackened, my bones honeycombed, my heart no longer used to pumping blood beyond the horizontal. I know the risks that come with inactivity, and that for me, any hospitalisation would be a searing agony, under the glare of fluorescent lights and the incomprehension of medical staff. I do not know what prolonged exposure to strong light would do to me now; it is quite possible that the reaction would prove fatal. I do not want to find out.

So I know that I must MOVE. Luckily, in the life before, I was a seeker after bodily truths. Low back pain, the result of falling off a bus, troubled me; in the end I found relief in Pilates and the Alexander technique.

Now I work on my core strength in the darkness. I pull in my lower abdominals after engaging my pelvic floor. I lie on my back with one knee bent and push the opposite heel vertically upwards, feeling my hamstring judder as it takes the unexpected strain. I exercise my quads by grasping one knee to my chest and extending the other leg horizontally to hover just above the carpet. I strengthen my shoulder girdle by performing the Plank, and practise Mexican waves with my toes. At other times I lie in the semi-supine position, knees bent, with my head on a couple of books, directing my back to lengthen and widen, and my knees to go forward and away.

Storm

I sit in the dark and listen to the storm. I hear the bitter clatter of rain against my walls, and the low boom of the wind, a strange unsettling frequency that makes bones in my skull vibrate.

A fiercer skirl of wind alters the rhythm of the rain. It rattles harder and faster against the walls, splats on to the windowpanes. The drip-drip-drip of an overflowing gutter starts up, then a second drip, out of kilter with the first. Unknown objects crash and roll in the street outside. A gate, ripped from its fastening, bangs back and forth, a maddening irregular handclap. The house itself is filled with cross-currents of air, which twitch along the frames of windows and suck at closed doors. The house shifts its weight around me, as if it were about to get to its feet and dance.

My ears exult in the glorious accumulating noise, my blood foams with the energy of the storm. The world outside is trying to reach me, roused from its usual indifference. It drags its claws along the bars of my cage. It puts its mouth to my walls, and roars.

My body has learnt to sit quietly in my room. It has learnt not to scream or sob or writhe. But my spirit swirls like the wind, surges like the rain. The wildness outside calls to the wildness within.

"I hear you," I cry out, in my mind. "I'm here, keep going, don't stop."

When the weather is filthy, it is natural to stay snug indoors. While the storm lasts, I have the illusion of normality. I can pretend I am inside my walls by choice, that I am merely waiting until the sky has cleared, and when it does I will walk out of the door and down the street, and breathe in the smell of soaked earth, and kick the toes of my boots through puddles, and watch droplets glide from shimmering leaves.

Slowly the rain loses its power, and the wind blows itself out. The house settles down around me and the cross-currents of air are stilled. Only the drip-drip of a gutter taps out a small coda to the vanished symphony; soon even that comes to an end.

Music

I have ears—why don't I listen to music?

And I have music, too: my CDs and tapes, brought with me from London, some lined up on the bottom shelf of the bureau within touching distance of where I sit, some mixed in with Pete's in a cabinet downstairs.

It is an eclectic collection. Brought up classical, I had a penchant for monumental choral and orchestral works—the complete Mahler symphonies, Beethoven's *Missa Solemnis*, the Bach B Minor Mass. I also liked chamber music that unites piano and strings in friendly combination, such as the "Archduke Trio" and the "Trout Quintet"—mellower and less austere than string quartets, or pianists on their own. As I grew older and left home, I acquired other favourites, each one introduced to me by a particular person at a particular time; taken together, a coded history of my previous life. There are albums by Pulp and the Waterboys, the Cowboy Junkies, ABBA and the Rolling Stones. There is even some AC/DC.

And inside my little radio, just a finger's push away, lurk endless unpredicted streams, in which you never know when your ears will come across something compelling, unexpected and new.

I have tried. But somehow, music listened to in solitary darkness becomes devastating in its power. Undiluted by other stimuli, it overwhelms the emotional centres of my brain so quickly, so completely, that only a few bars are necessary to dissolve my careful stoicism into wild tears.

This is the effect of all music, any music, music I have loved, music I have never heard before. The curls and twists of melody, the simplest alternation of chords, are probing fingers in my mind, pulling the lids off memories, tearing the shrouds from impossible yearnings, beaming floodlights on to departed joys. Music unhinges me, reduces to howling chaos my prudent tidying of emotion, my management of agony.

I do not wish to writhe on the floor of my room in paroxysms of weeping. It is pointless and unaesthetic, makes me hot and bothered, doesn't help my skin. So I forgo the liquid pleasures of music, which serve only to flood me with things I have lost, and choose instead the dry pebbles of words.

Dream 2

I am sitting up in bed in a strange room. The walls are covered in intensely floral wallpaper—a pattern of pink roses crowding together on a cream background. My bed is a single, and I look down its length to a window, through which there is a misty Scottish landscape—a small angle of garden fringed with orange montbretia, and penned in by rough stone walls—and beyond it, grey and purple moorland muted by white haze.

The room smells of old furniture, musty bedding, soft rain, worn carpet, well-thumbed detective novels and dust. It is the smell of a place not in permanent occupation, but with all that is needed for temporary happiness. I realise I am in a bedroom from my childhood, in the cottage we rented for family holidays, year after year.

In the bed I am propped up on pillows and I am holding something that weighs heavily on my arms.

I look down, and see that it is a baby, and I know that it is mine, and that I have recently given birth. The baby has pale skin and large brown eyes, like my own. It also has a head of the most astonishing red hair, pure unvariegated flame. I am surprised, and wonder where the hair has come from. But then I remember photographs of Pete's brother David when he was young, with hair that was the same glowing, traffic-light red.

Not so implausible then, I think, this baby. And as I wake, and it dissolves, I remember the time when it was not implausible in real life, the time after the first disaster but before the second, the run of months that promised so much, a period of adjustment, and of hope.

October 2005

The woman looks at me nervously as I sit down on the opposite seat. She places her arm protectively around the small child at her side. "It's OK," I say, in a friendly way, "I'm not infectious. I've just got a light sensitivity condition, that's all."

It is October, and I am on the train to London for my appointment with a dermatologist, at last. I am wearing a dark red coat, an oversized cap with a big peak in a burgundy woollen fabric and a mask I have made myself. I cut it from a dark red satin scarf, using a double layer for improved light protection, hemming it neatly, and attaching a piece of elastic each side to hook over my ears. It covers my nose, mouth and cheeks. However, it does become damp and stuffy under the satin, and my spectacles steam up. Periodically, I pull the mask down for a while, in order to cool off. The whole ensemble co-ordinates well.

The woman opposite ignores my friendly remarks. After staring at me suspiciously, she looks out of the window for five minutes as the train trundles through undistinguished suburbs under a flat grey sky. Then, casually, as if the thought had only just occurred to her, she picks up her child and walks to the other end of the carriage.

I shake my head and smile behind my mask. I am becoming used to strange reactions to my garb, which I now must wear every time I go outdoors, unless I wait till dusk. It does not help, of course, that this is October 2005, three months after the 7/7 bombings, and everyone is on high alert for suspicious characters on the transport system. My close friend Jonathan was in the underground carriage next to the bomb at Aldgate—he escaped with only a badly jarred spine, but he can no longer handle his commute into town. "I saw things that no one should ever see," is all he says on the subject, but in the night, he screams.

We are falling out of the labour market together, in a graceful backward arc, he with a diagnosis of post-traumatic stress disorder, I with my mysterious skin. We compare notes by phone on the HR departments of our employers as, slowly and inexorably, long-term sickness absence moves towards careful, procedurally correct dismissals.

Since July, I have been living in Itchingford with Pete. I have been eating healthily, and taking exercise. I have been going for runs through the estate in the summer evenings, smelling the twilight fragrances and coming continually upon cats, sitting enigmatically on gateposts, draped along kerbstones or shooting silently across my path. Investigating Pete's bookshelves, I have been reading novels I didn't know before—*Darkness at Noon* by Arthur Koestler, Joseph Heller's *Catch-22* and the thrillers of Adam Hall. I have cleaned the house, and done our collective washing, and experimented with recipes from cookery books I've had for years but never used.

And I have begun to wonder if, perhaps, the loss of everything I thought defined me—my career, my independence, the freedom to go where I want in the world—is not in fact the loss of self I feared. I have been finding parts of me squashed and crumpled, like favourite clothes that have fallen down the back of a chest of drawers and been forgotten, and now I have the chance to smooth them out and hold them to the light.

I know I do not have much courage. If this had not happened, despite wondering, periodically, about life beyond the civil service, I would have stayed on that escalator until the end, never quite having the guts to climb over the side. Now, with this brutal shove, I'm being given the chance to see a different me develop, while perhaps, somewhere in another part of the multiverse, a dedicated policy expert keeps trudging into the office, growing hoary and experienced in the subtleties of power.

I had been obsessed with my flat, with the need to make my space and live in it on my own. But over the summer just gone, I have discovered that living with Pete has been . . . well, fun. The realisation came to me quite suddenly, one lunchtime, as I looked across the table and found the space before my eyes filled with his form, and something lifted up inside me, like a secret inner smile.

I am thinking over this strange heightened summer as the train pulls into Clapham Junction. As I move through the crowd on the platform, a young woman looks at my mask and mutters behind her hand to her friend: "Just like Michael Jackson!" I smile again under the clammy material. "Well, I never knew that," I say to myself. "So—I have a celebrity accessory. Was it too much plastic surgery in his case, I wonder, or was he just worried about germs?"

The appointment itself is an anticlimax. The dermatologist listens to my story and examines my face under her special magnifying lamp. "I do not like the look of this," she says. "But this is not my area of expertise. I am going to refer you to a specialist photobiology unit."

It takes another few weeks. And when I first go there, it is simply for various biochemical tests. I provide samples of blood, urine and stools, wrapped immediately in silver foil to limit light exposure (they will be checking for porphyria, among other conditions, and the relevant chemicals decay quickly on contact with light). They tell me that I will be sent an appointment for light testing, some time in the spring.

November 2005

Pete has the first full week of November off work, because it is Tree Week—the period when autumn colour is at its most splendid, and therefore most worthy of a photographer's time and attention.

Of course, Tree Week can vary depending on climatic conditions—if it has been blowing a gale, most of the leaves can be gone. Or, if the weather has been mild, a number of trees may not have fully turned. But employers do not grant photographers spontaneous tree leave—everything has to be booked in advance. The first full week of November proves to be right more often than not.

"How did you get on at Winkworth Arboretum?" I ask, when Pete returns one afternoon, humping tripod and camera gear in from the car.

"It was great," he enthuses. "There weren't many people about, so I was able to get out my central column."

I laugh in a coarse and lewd manner.

"Really," he says severely. "The young ladies of today. That was a perfectly legitimate photographic remark."

As all serious photographers will know, the central column is the extra pole in the middle of a tripod which can be extended upwards, above the legs, to gain additional height. The language of photography is rich in such stimulating metaphors. It is not uncommon to talk about "taking a second body," or "keeping my old legs but getting a new head." Shooting in large format requires a rising front, whilst those who use digital boast about the spectacular size of their sensors.

"My plan is to go to the New Forest on Friday," says Pete. "Would you like to come with me, if your face is feeling up to it?"

I eagerly accept. I've never been to the New Forest, apart from once to a wildlife park for the purpose of seeing wild boar, for which I have always had a soft spot, after reading all the Asterix books when young. The boar stalked about in a stately way, thrusting their long snouts into the churned-up ground. The interpretative board on the fence of their large wooded enclosure praised their high intelligence and low cunning, their ability to run fast, swim rivers and elude pursuit. Since ancient times, it went on, hunting them was considered an extremely hazardous and therefore highly prestigious activity. I was pleased to find myself a fan of such a superior creature.

On Friday morning, however, we are on the hunt for other things. We bound down the A339 as it dips and surges between two smooth walls of trunks.

"Look out for a turning on the right with a sign for Bolderwood," says Pete.

"There, there!" I shout.

We swerve off on to a single-track road that tunnels

into the trees. Inside the car, the light goes dim. The sounds of traffic on the main road die away, and soon all we can hear is the scrunch of our own tyres and the engine's purr, loud in the leafy silence. It is as though we are being absorbed into an enormous living organism; if I were to look back and see the forest close in, amoeba-like, behind us, I would not be surprised.

Time stretches. For what seems hours, but must only be minutes, there is nothing but our gentle forward motion under the upraised arms of the trees.

Finally we stop in a small gravelled parking bay to the side of the road. I get out and look up to a sudden slice of brilliant white sky. The air prickles as I inhale, like sparkling water. Pete opens the boot and extracts his gear. "I'm glad I bought this lightweight tripod," he says. "It's much easier to lug about."

I sing him a chorus from Handel's *Messiah*, with photographic words: "His yoke is easy and his tripod is light."

We cross the empty single-track road and set off down a sandy track whiskered with bright green grass. Across it is a low wooden bar, about knee height, to prevent the entry of motor vehicles. "Shall I leap?" I say to Pete. "I haven't done anything like this since we did high jump at primary school, with poles and bamboo canes."

"Well, it's up to you," he says, "but try not to go flat on your face at the outset. That would be unfortunate."

"I'll be prudent," I say, stepping over the bar.

The path snakes along as though at the bottom of a canyon, a pale sandy stripe mirroring a pale strip of sky. The trees are huge and intensely individual—fat, gnarled, tan-leaved oaks, smooth columnar beeches with their peachy, biscuity foliage, golden birches and sweet chestnuts, the occasional sober-suited conifer, refusing to be drawn in. Leaves crunch under our feet; now and again there is a rustling off to the side as some creature passes on its way.

"Now here's a fine tree," Pete says, as we come to a large beech set slightly back from the path, which thrusts one of its muscular grey limbs out sideways, exactly parallel to the ground. The limb runs straight for a couple of metres before curving upwards, creating a perfect seat.

I plunge through ankle-deep leaves and settle myself on the accommodating arm. "This is great," I say happily. "Just the right height." It's shady on the branch, under the multi-layered canopy. I unhook my mask and stuff it in the pocket of my coat. Pete sets up his camera on its tripod, then comes towards me and takes my hand.

"You know I love you ever so much, don't you?"

My heart drops through my body, as though a hangman had kicked away its stool. Oh God, I think, why do men do this? Why do they organise a nice day out, take you to a beautiful place, tell you that they love you—then explain that for various subtle and complicated reasons, you also have to break up.

I take a last breath of sparkling air, and brace myself against the tree.

"Will you marry me?" he says.

For a few moments I am completely stunned. I stare

at him, round-eyed. Then a cascade of mad mixed-up thoughts bursts through my head, whirling in wild eddies, throwing off question marks like fine spray. I don't know what to say. "Are you sure?" are the words that come to the front of my mind. For we have reached this point by such a bizarre and unpropitious route, there must be a million reasons why it cannot be a good idea. Yet maybe this is part of the true pattern of life—one of the unlooked-for consequences that arise from its ferocious twists and turns, a strange new compound formed inexplicably inside its crucible of pain.

In my mind, planets collide, civilisations evolve and decay. Like petals of a giant flower, possible worlds unfold. In reality, only seconds pass. I still do not know what to say; in the end my mouth speaks for me; it says:

"Yes."

December 2005

"I suppose I could retrain as a plumber," I say doubtfully.

"I'm not sure that would be a good idea," says Pete. "You'd need to be able to lift a bath."

We are sitting at the table, replete with Sunday lunch, considering what kind of work I might be able to do, and attempting to think outside the box. The challenge is to find something that does not take place in modern office environments, does not involve spending too long out of doors, and does not require extended periods under fluorescent lights.

"It's got to be some sort of personal service," I say, "where I control the surroundings and people come to see me."

"Psychotherapy or counselling," suggests Pete.

"I wouldn't be any good at that at all," I reply firmly. "Absolutely not. What about reflexology or kinesiology or some sort of complementary health thing?"

It is Pete's turn to look sceptical.

"Prostitute!" I say. "One of the discreet, suburban kind."

"Suppose we try a different approach," says Pete. "Apart from develop and implement government policy, what can you actually do?"

"Er, play the piano?"

"There you are, then."

"You mean teach it?" He nods. "Do you know," I say, "that is not a completely silly idea, and it had crossed my mind. It would be a bit weird, kind of like entering the family business, but it could be good fun."

"Well, it seems the most realistic, darling."

So I look into the matter, and discover that some people set up as piano teachers without any specific qualifications at all, beyond some grade exams, and then learn on the job. But I do not have sufficient chutzpah to do this. Being a bureaucratic soul, I know I will feel much more confident if I have done a training course and got a certificate.

I also discover that the European Piano Teachers' Association (UK branch) runs a piano pedagogy course that starts in January, and involves going to the Royal College of Music every second Sunday for six months. Given the state of my face, this would be difficult, but just about achievable. I qualify to go on the course, because I have passed my Grade 8 (when I was seventeen) and have been playing pieces of diploma level since. The deadline for enrolment is looming, and I am feeling keen and motivated, so I decide to sign up—but there is one snag. In order actually to be assessed and therefore qualify for a certificate, I am expected to have procured two students on whom to try out what I will be learning from week to week. For each student, there are lesson plans to be prepared, a lesson diary to be kept and an extended essay to be written about their progress.

The course is aimed at a wide range of levels of experience, so, for those participants who already have a teaching practice, this does not present a problem. However, I am new and green, and therefore have somehow to lasso two pupils from the local community, from a standing start, before the middle of January, which is in about four weeks.

I design an advert. "Have you always wanted to learn the piano?" it says. "I am looking for two students to take part in a teaching project." Pete photoshops the text white on black, with a piano keyboard running up one side, and we distribute copies around the neighbourhood in local shops and the library. Nobody does anything over the festive season, so I settle down to enjoy Christmas, and hope I will get some replies in the New Year, when people peel themselves off the sofa, and start to look about them.

Christmas 2005

I am in charge of Christmas dinner!

It is the first Christmas that Pete and I have spent together. I am looking forward to being the person delegating tasks rather than one of the hapless delegatees, required to hang about looking helpful and making periodic offers to peel sprouts.

I have drawn up a Project Plan, which indicates at what times various activities need to happen, in order to meet the objective of lunch at half-past one. (I find this very satisfying, and it is indeed similar to what I used to do in the civil service. Clearly I am missing work . . .)

We have invited my mother and brother, Sam, who arrive on one of the last trains out of south-west London before everything shuts down. My father is not with us, having died a few years before. He and my mother divorced when I was fifteen, a great surprise for my brother and me. We had a very happy childhood full of jokes, laughter and affection, with no tensions evident between our parents until my father fell in love with someone else.

On Christmas morning, I am up at eight o'clock to get the turkey out of the fridge. Soon my mother comes in, in her dressing gown. "Hello, my best daughter," she says. "Happy Xmas. Now mind what you're doing with that turkey. Are there any oats?" Both my mother and my brother, although living independently, are on a healthy eating kick.

"In the cupboard," I say. "Pete got some specially."

My mother prepares a large bowl of oats and chopped apple. Then she goes back into the living room, sits down at the piano and breaks into an extempore version of "Merry Christmas Everybody" by Slade, thus ensuring that everyone else is also awake.

Soon creaking and sloshing from upstairs indicate that my brother is having his morning shower, about which he is always very thorough, so that afterwards the bathroom looks as if someone has been trying to wash a baby elephant; plastic bottles of shampoo upended and squeezed in the middle, water on every available surface, towels and bathmat askew.

"Morning, Sam," I say to him when he comes down. "How's tricks?"

"Not too bad, thanks. Are there any oats?" I point them out. When he has finished his breakfast, he sits down at the piano and does an alternative version of "Merry Christmas Everybody," all slow gloopy chords and dramatic modulations, because it is in the style of Brahms, who is his favourite composer. He finishes off with a fugue.

"Very good, Sam," says Pete, who has come down, having attempted a modest lie-in after going to Midnight Mass. "But could we have something other than Slade?"

"Oh sorry," says Sam, always sweet-natured and obliging. He begins a series of variations on "Hark! the Herald Angels Sing" in various musical styles, including baroque and blues.

It will have become obvious by this point why, although a competent pianist myself, I have always felt intimidated by the extreme facility of my mother and brother, particularly when it comes to improvising. They also have very good musical memories and perfect pitch.

"Right," says my mother, bouncing back into the living room after having a bath. "Now, what shall I do in respect of lunch? And when are we going to have presents?" She enters the kitchen just as I am lifting the turkey out of the oven to baste it. "Stop!" she yells, aghast, and I nearly drop the roasting tray. "That does not look at all good for the back. Can't you get Pete to lift it in and out? And that oven is very badly designed. I've always said you ought to get the door rehung, so that it opens sideways, like mine."

"Mum, I'm doing fine," I say, putting the bird on the worktop. "Just don't come up behind me and make a loud noise."

"Oh all right, but you should think about that oven door. Shall I start peeling potatoes?"

"Well, we don't have to do that until ten fifteen and there's some other things I need to concentrate on first. And I thought we'd have presents at eleven o'clock, once I've got the spuds in the oven."

"What about sprouts?"

"We're not having sprouts. We kind of thought— neither of us like them, so we'd have broccoli."

"Hmmm. I rather like sprouts. A very traditional winter vegetable."

Sam wanders in, looking helpful. "Can I chop something?" he enquires.

I am becoming flustered. I foresee that unless I provide some sort of distraction to keep people out of the kitchen until I need them, something is going to go wrong.

Pete realises what is happening and nudges me. "Didn't you want these two to have a look at 'Little Donkey'?" he says.

This is a brainwave. In the run-up to Christmas, Alex, a friend of ours, had asked me if I would make an arrangement of the children's carol with an easy piano part so that she could accompany her daughters, who had to learn it for school. I wrote out the melody for the right hand and added some basic chords underneath, even developing a clip-clop bass line, of which I was rather proud. The exercise made my brain feel stretched in unusual directions, because I had not thought about harmony for years. Alex was pleased with the result, and she and her daughters performed it to me over the telephone, with gusto. However, I would also like some feedback from the experts.

My mother and brother become immediately alert. Their spines lengthen and their noses twitch. Pete leads them to the piano, and indicates the small manuscript book in which I have written out my masterwork.

For the next hour, two ferocious musical intelligences are trained upon this modest arrangement.

"There is an implied consecutive fifth between the first and second bar," says one.

"I'd say the C in the bass is far enough away from the D not to matter," says the other. "However, the use of the supertonic chord in bar two is weak. I would prefer a subdominant."

"Well, what about bars five and six? Now that is a *serious* implied consecutive octave."

"Yes, there ought to be G followed by A in the bass, rather than E followed by F. That gives a nice bass line and circumvents the problem."

"And in bar six, one would swap the harmonies round."

At times, the debate becomes heated.

Pete and I get on with the Project Plan, seething with suppressed giggles whenever we catch each other's eye.

Lunch is delivered on time and pronounced a success. The verdict on "Little Donkey" is that what I wrote was mostly OK, but that improvements could be introduced at various points, if I wish to make it truly rigorous.

In the afternoon, we have a game of Scrabble, which my mother wins, with two seven-letter words.

January 2006

Very soon in the New Year, I have my first piano pupil. She is Libby, a sober, intelligent ten-year-old, with googly blue eyes and straight pale hair. Her mother wants her to "have the opportunity to try lots of things, to see if she likes them." She is already doing football and French, and learning the recorder.

Having made such a good start, I am sanguine about finding a second student, but the days tick by and the telephone is maddeningly silent. I reread the rubric supplied by the course. Yes—definitely two students—and furthermore, two *contrasting* students, each posing different pedagogical challenges.

I begin to look at my fiancé with a speculative air.

A few days before the start of the course, Pete is relaxing on the sofa after a day at work, reading a bit of the Saturday paper. "Pete," I say, "could I ask you a huge favour?"

"What sort of favour?"

"Look, I'm really sorry about this, I wouldn't ask if I had any other options, but . . . you know I've only got one student?"

"Yes."

"And if I don't have two students, I could end up doing the whole course and not getting the certificate, which would be really frustrating."

"Yes."

"Well, I was wondering—would you be my other student?"

"What?" He looks sharply up from his newspaper.

"Would you be my other student, and let me teach you the piano—just for a few months, for the duration of the course?"

"What, me—learn the piano?"

"Er—yes."

"But . . . I can't even read music."

"I'll teach you. That'd be part of it."

"But . . . what would I have to do?"

"Well, I'd give you a lesson every week, and in between you'd need to practise."

"Practise?"

"Yes—just a little bit, most days . . ."

"I'm not practising if there's footie on the telly."

"No, no, of course not," I say hastily. "It doesn't have to be absolutely every day."

"Hmmm. I don't think I'd be any good."

"That doesn't matter, at all. Anyway, you don't know that, until you try it."

And, eventually, he agrees.

I lean down and put my arms round him, resting my face against his hair.

"Thank you, my darling," I say. "I'm sorry everything is so bonkers, and that this is yet another bonkers thing."

THE COURSE TAKES place in a large high-ceilinged room, on the third floor of the Royal College of Music's Victorian building, which looks out through two tall windows on to South Kensington rooftops and sky. I reach a deal with the tutors and the other participants: we will keep the fluorescent lights in the room off, unless it is especially dull or dark outside. However, there are also a number of distinguished visiting lecturers, who blow in to deliver one-off sessions on "Psychology for the Piano Teacher" or "Composition and Musical Form." They are to make their own decisions about the lights. So if a lecturer bounces in saying breezily, "Now, let's have some light on the proceedings, shall we?" it is my cue to squirm quietly backwards into the dimmest corner of the room, and put on my hat and mask.

The small kitchen a couple of floors down where we eat lunch and have coffee is cramped and dark, and needs to be lit. I am in a quandary every time we have a break: do I accompany the others, unmask, eat, drink, be sociable and get pain; accompany the others, not eat or drink, and attempt to be sociable through my mask while they consume coffee and sandwiches (always a slightly odd proceeding); or do I withdraw to some quiet, unlit room, and eat by myself, in the undemanding company of one or two grand pianos, as they stalk across pale carpet on elegantly turned legs?

I try all of these over the weeks, in combination and succession. My unusual situation places a strange invisible barrier between me and the other participants, a sort of subtle thickening of the air, through which social interactions, in either direction, find it harder to pass.

It becomes by far the most stressful part of the course.

February 2006

Pete has been having piano lessons for five weeks. I have planned each one carefully, and written a report on how it went for my course file.

Teaching a fully grown mathematical type is indeed different from teaching a ten-year-old girl. When I introduce him to middle C, he says, "Why isn't it middle A? That would be more logical." My attempts to answer this question lead to a long discussion about the principles of tonality, the diatonic scale, the development of clefs and the harmonic ratios between notes in terms of oscillations per second. Which is not exactly what I had planned for Lesson 2.

Pete is quite good about practising. I try to keep out

of the way as much as possible, and go for a run when I can. I remember too well what it was like growing up, trying to practise in the same house as my mother who was also my teacher—not always an easy combination. Occasionally, provoked beyond endurance by some continually perpetuated fault, she would burst into the piano room saying, "No, no, you've lost the middle line, allow me to demonstrate," and sweep me from the stool. Alternatively, when I had finished, and come out into the kitchen, she would produce some classic remark such as "You're doing some jolly good work on that Chopin. I like the way you're trying to get it in time, too."

I did most of my practice in the early morning, with the thick velvet curtains of the garden-facing piano room tightly drawn, and my parents asleep upstairs at the front of the house.

Now, in Itchingford, it is about eight o'clock in the evening. Pete is practising the piano and I am in the office, trying not to listen as he blunders through the same phrase over and over again. "You are NOT going to go downstairs," I tell myself firmly, and concentrate hard on *The Perfect Wrong Note*, a radical book about music learning that I am reading for my course. The botched repetition continues. I grit my teeth. But it does no good. There is something weirdly zombified about what he is doing. He is wasting effort, and probably getting fed up. I have to intervene—it will be better in the longer run.

So I hurry downstairs and open the living-room door.

Pete is sitting at the piano, splodging through his

piece for the fiftieth time. But there is another noise as well, a sort of mixed humming and buzzing, which at first I cannot identify at all.

Then I catch sight of a small silver radio perched on top of the piano, its slim shiny aerial extended to maximum length. All at once, what I am hearing makes total sense.

Pete is practising, but he is also listening to a football match on Radio 5 Live.

"PETE!" I say loudly. "What on earth are you doing?"

He stops playing and looks round. "Er . . . I was sort of multi-tasking," he replies, sheepishly.

"Pete," I say, exasperated. "Honestly, it's not worth it. You'll get much more benefit from ten minutes' practice if you're really concentrating, than from half an hour going round in circles because you're listening to the football at the same time. Believe me, it's not efficient."

"Oh all right, point taken," he says, switching off the radio.

"Look, you've probably done enough for tonight anyway. Why don't you just stop and listen to the match?"

So he does.

As it turns out, when it comes to Pete's progress on the piano, football is not entirely unhelpful. I find the following written in his piano notebook, as a practice exercise in the notation of rhythm:

68

Here we go here we go here we go

February 2006—Later

Pete and I set about organising a wedding. The plan is to find a hotel in the vicinity where the civil ceremony can take place, go to Pete's church for a blessing (he is a Christian, I am not) and then come back to the hotel for the reception.

We check out various venues, and the one that looks most promising is a hotel called The Manor, a long, rambling, two-storey building, set in pleasant grounds. Tall plane trees line the drive, their sturdy bases sunk in carpets of crocuses sticking out golden tongues to the early spring sun.

Inside, the hotel has rich brown panelling, a sage-green carpet, faded chintz upholstery and gold-framed paintings on the walls. It even has old-fashioned lighting—modest chandeliers and unpretentious sconces fitted, brilliantly, as far as I am concerned, with incandescent bulbs.

The whole effect is mellow and relaxing. It even smells right—no discordant notes of new furniture, or industrial detergent, or frying.

A friendly receptionist, soft and beige and rosy, shows us into a sunny sitting room, and we wait on flowery armchairs, on opposite sides of a low table with carved paw-like feet, smiling at each other, because we know we've found the place.

Then we meet Celia, the wedding co-ordinator.

Celia has jet-black hair that reaches midway down her back, a bony, angular body and black eyebrows drawn together in a semi-permanent scowl. She is wearing shiny black court shoes with finely pointed toes, and stands before us, arms crossed across a file, legs apart and spiky feet splayed outwards, like daggers. There is a patch of high colour on each of her cheeks.

We tell her we really like the hotel, and are thinking of getting married in September. "No," she says. "You can't do that. You'll have to go later in the year. September's gone."

"But—we rang this morning and they told us the ninth is still free."

"Who told you that?"

"I don't know—whoever I spoke to—the receptionist?"

Celia clicks her tongue and snorts. "Oh. Well, it might be, but if it is, it'll be the only one."

"And we were thinking of ninety guests for a sit-down meal."

"You can't have ninety," Celia snaps. "You can have forty-five in the Oak Room, or seventy in the Garden Room. Or you can have a fork buffet for one hundred and ten."

"Well . . ." I say, "supposing we used both rooms. There's quite a wide connecting doorway. We could have close family and friends in the Oak Room, with us, and everyone else in the other one, and keep the doors open."

Celia's eyebrows surge downwards into a savage V, and her eyes flash. "There aren't enough tables," she counters. "They would have to be hired in."

"But that would be possible, wouldn't it? We'd pay the extra cost."

Grudgingly she admits that tables can be hired, and makes a grim note in her file.

"Then, we'd like some dancing."

It turns out that the hotel has a disco with a small dance floor, and it can be set up at one end of the Garden Room.

"Actually, we were thinking more of a barn dance or ceilidh, with a caller, and people sort of dancing up and down the whole length of the room—"

"You can't do that," says Celia. "There would be health and safety issues with the carpet."

Extensive and subtle cross-questioning is required in order to establish that there will be no health and safety issues if we can track down and hire a dance floor that will cover the whole of the carpet in the Garden Room. Pete thinks such things are of modular construction and can be made bigger or smaller quite easily, to fit.

This evidence of lateral thinking makes Celia fume. Her pointed toes splay savagely and the spots on her cheeks turn purple.

Naively, I had assumed that when you entered upon the business of having a wedding, service providers would lay themselves out to meet your requirements, safe in the knowledge that you had clearly decided to spend some money, and that they could therefore charge you hefty fees to make it worth their while. But Celia does not operate on this principle. She believes in the relentless disciplining of dreams.

In the car afterwards, Pete and I look at each other. "Blimey," he says, leaning back against the headrest and taking a deep breath.

"What an extraordinary person," I say faintly.

But we persist, because the hotel is so nice, and the lighting is suitable, and everyone else we have dealings with there is lovely and amenable. Celia continues to be erratically obstructive and unpleasant, and proves impossible to get hold of on the phone. When I speak to the bar manager and agree some minor point about the drinks, Celia is furious. "You should not have made any arrangement with her," she shouts. "She has no supervisory authority." When we turn up at the hotel for a pre-arranged meeting, we find that Celia has gone home.

"She's not really into customer service, is she?" says Pete.

"I think she's in the wrong job. She doesn't seem to like weddings much."

"She doesn't seem to like people much."

Gradually we get the details sorted out, but I have disturbing premonitions about the day itself, a recurring vision of Celia striding down the hotel steps, black hair flying, palm upraised, shouting, "No! You can't come in."

———

IN THE END, the wedding does not happen, but for this, Celia is not to blame. Other, stranger forces wreck our plans; to that extent my premonitions prove correct.

Games to Play in the Dark 2: Circle of Words

For this game you need a companion. But it is a relaxed, co-operative sort of game, with no winners or losers.

Think of a compound word or phrase—like Football, or Flower Power, or Hot Potato. Then, using the second part of the word or phrase, add something on to make a new word or phrase.

elephant's foot ball + chain mail fraudster crazy horse sense sible Fawlty wiring diagram attic bedroom window box + cox apple pie crust acean

Take it in turns. Keep going until you link back to the original word.

Active encouragement is given to homonyms, chutzpah, surreal flights of fancy and appalling puns.

SAS

I have made an interesting discovery. I really like SAS thrillers.

Once I had a thrusting Liverpudlian boss, who strode about saying, "*Bravo Two Zero*—best management textbook ever written." But that was the limit of my knowledge of the genre, until my book collector procured one from the local library.

I am hooked. What's so great about SAS thrillers is the amount of useful, practical, how-to information they contain, about all sorts of things. I have learnt, for example, that SAS members always keep one eye shut when looking at a map at night. It takes forty minutes for the human eye to adjust fully to darkness; keeping one shut ensures you don't lose all your night vision when you turn on a torch. (I can well believe the forty minutes. Sometimes it's only after I've sat for a while in my room that I start to notice a crack in the curtains or a line at the base of the door.)

I have learnt how to live in a bush for several days, keeping observation on a target. I have discovered that the necessary equipment includes secateurs, gardening gloves, camouflage netting, cling film, Imodium, a petrol can and food that doesn't make a noise. I have learnt that breaking someone's neck requires a screwing action, similar to getting the lid off a jar of jam. I have learnt how to cover my scent when being tracked by dogs, and how to strip off and make a raft to swim a river, so that I have dry clothes to wear on the other side.

It is all fascinating—and very pleasant and stimulating, especially as I am in a situation where acquiring new skills is pretty near impossible. So I enjoy my theoretical survival lessons; the fact that I am probably, out of the entire human race, the person least qualified to join the SAS, and the person least likely ever to have a use for these skills, doesn't bother me.

There is a thought experiment favoured by philosophers who worry about the foundations of human knowledge: if you were a brain in a bucket, and all your sensory experiences were created in you by the sophisticated equipment of a mad scientist, would you be able to tell?

The technology that stimulates my brain is crude, utilising only one of my sensory channels (the auditory nerves), and strongly dependent on my store of memories and impressions from the life before. But it nonetheless has some effect, as I move stealthily towards my objective, crawling on my belly through earth and undergrowth, a pistol in my hand and a knife in my belt.

I can, in my darkness, live so many different lives.

Strangely, there is one thing we have in common, these SAS heroes and I: the degree of effort we direct to the management of risk. Before an operation, the SAS prepare meticulously, researching the objective to the best of their ability. They try to ascertain the timing of guard patrols around the perimeter fence, the position of the exits, the number and the firepower of the enemy. They think through different scenarios, and work out what they will do in each hypothetical situation. Finally, they check and check and recheck their equipment to make sure that it is working, that it can be brought out swiftly, that they know exactly in which pocket each item is stowed. All risks that can be minimised are minimised, before they enter a red sector.

In the life before, I walked up Scottish mountains without a first-aid kit, and, occasionally, on my own. Sometimes I waded small rivers, if I needed to get to the other side. Once, I visited a friend in Biggleswade, and, wanting to reach the continuation of a footpath, we ran hand in hand across the A1—a wild exhilarating dash over four lanes, with cars zooming at us at seventy miles per hour.

But these were calculated risks. I exercised my judgement on each set of circumstances, weighed the possible consequences, and decided that I was much more likely to be all right than not.

Now I have given up such grand gestures. I am in a permanent red sector, and am intensely aware, all the time, of the enormity of the downside risk, the abyss that awaits me, should anything go wrong. I select with great care the chair I will stand on to get down a plate from a high shelf in the kitchen, checking and rechecking the wobbliness of its seat. I clean my teeth twice a day, counting up to the recommended two minutes, and floss with dedication, hoping to forestall decay. For some reason I am always getting into difficulties with chicken, frequently phoning my mother to pose some variant of the following: "Mum, Pete cooked some chicken on Saturday lunchtime, and then left it out of the fridge until the evening to cool down, and then it was in the fridge for two days—should I eat it?"

"Yes, hello," she says. "This is the Chicken Advisory Service speaking." The Advisory Service always gives clear and definitive advice.

At his work, Pete was taught a mantra on a health and safety course: "Think 'what if,' not 'if only,'" and I do. Caution infects all my movements now, and all my small decisions in the black and in the gloom.

And I must not get pregnant.

Now there is something that does not worry the SAS.

Telephone Friends

I have got to know other people in the strange club of the chronically ill. I have friends I talk to on the phone but have never met; friends who are at home during the day, at home, in fact, nearly all of the time. Like me, they had a life before that has been lost; now they wander in the twilight zone where doctors diagnose but cannot cure, and the faint miasma of societal suspicion, never attached to those with cancer, or with heart disease, hangs about them, that somehow it must all be psychosomatic, or that at a deep level they actually want to be ill.

How did we find each other? Bizarrely, the European Union is mostly responsible: its plan for a compulsory switch to compact fluorescent light bulbs in homes and offices—in fact, everywhere—causes deep concern among people with a range of health conditions who find these bulbs give them painful and severe reactions. (Not everyone with a particular condition is affected this way—nothing so elegant, helpful or uncomplicated—just a subset, in each case.) Trying to find out what is happening, discussing how to influence UK MPs (mostly lovely and supportive) and the European Commission (the equivalent, it will sadly turn out, of smashing your face against granite), and sharing information about possible alternatives that may not be banned, I speak to people with ME and lupus and other conditions, and we put each other in touch with more.

With some, I just talk about light bulbs, and that is the end of the matter. With others, I start off talking about light bulbs, and we end up talking about our shared experience of falling away from the normal, about books and families and politics and ideas; we keep on talking.

My telephone friends speak of pain, debility and nausea, of fatigue and fog in the brain—but in absolute terms, their activities, unfouled by the darkness, are less restricted than my own.

Down the telephone wires my friends give me massive transfusions of life. I come off the phone, every time, more cheerful than before.

Tales of Telephone Friends 1: Véronique

Véronique is one telephone friend whom I did know in person in the life before. I met her when she came from France to study for a year in the UK. Always a brilliant girl, in the league tables so favoured by the French, she invariably finished high, receiving the best marks in the country for her baccalaureate and hoping for an elevated position in the national examination which must be taken by all, in France, who wish to work in museums.

Fascinated by objects since her childhood, Véronique specialised in the art of the Pacific Islands. But her curatorial dreams were destroyed by long spells of depression, which then began to alternate with manic crises. She became familiar with the insides of psychiatric institutions, and was eventually diagnosed with bipolar disease.

"This morning I have been to see my shrink," Véronique says, on the telephone. "The appointment is only fifteen minutes, so one has to talk very fast. He is not ideal, my shrink, but he is the only behaviourist in my city."

I ask Véronique if there are charities in France that support people with mental health problems.

"There is a charity to support the *relatives* of people with mental health problems," Véronique says, "to help them cope with the stigma." She often talks about her dilemma, as she tries to meet new people, over what she should tell them about her condition. Merely to admit that she is not working can provoke a surprising degree of moral condemnation; if she then reveals the reason, the reactions range from horrified withdrawal to the advocacy of New Age therapies, instructions to pull herself together, because everyone has mood swings, or a recommendation to submit herself to the Roman Catholic Church. Friendly, polite and keen to please, Véronique finds it difficult to give her interlocutors a suitably robust response.

Véronique attends various adult education classes, ". . . but they are very female—the only people I meet are elderly ladies!"

"What classes are you going to?" I ask.

"Ceramics, life-drawing," says Véronique, "and Tai Chi."

"Perhaps you should try something with more appeal to men. What about a walking group?"

"I have joined a walking group, but it also consists only of ladies."

Véronique and I speculate regarding what French men might be doing, as they certainly are not attending adult education classes.

Eventually Véronique solves the problem by joining an Internet group called "*On va sortir,*" where people link up to go to concerts, exhibitions and so on.

One day she announces that she has met a young man called Nicolas, a counsellor and therapist. Relationship counselling is one of his specialities.

"He has classic Alsatian good looks," says Véronique, who, as a native of Alsace, frequently uses this adjective.

I really should be used to it by now, but I cannot help myself: every time Véronique says it, large brown dogs with pointed ears lope across the display screen of my mind.

"For our third date," says Véronique, "he asked me to go with him to a sauna in Germany. There was a sign on the wall telling people not to talk, so we sat on our towels in a huge room, in silence, surrounded by naked Germans. It was spooky."

"So . . . were you naked as well?" I ask faintly, feeling very buttoned-up and English.

"Oh yes, but that's quite normal. In French saunas everyone is naked, but at least one is able to chat."

It is for the joy of such unexpected vignettes that I am indebted to Véronique.

It soon becomes clear that Nicolas is more interested in analysing their relationship than in having it; specifically he is interested in improving Véronique so that she becomes a more suitable partner for him. Even eager-to-please Véronique realises this is rather one-sided, and they part.

Véronique's English is very good, but every so often she struggles to find an exact translation, or I use an English idiom that she does not understand. We have great fun working out the French equivalents for "white lies" (*pieux mensonges*), "public spending cuts" (*la rigueur*), "champagne socialist" (*la gauche caviar*) and many other fine expressions.

Tales of Telephone Friends 2:
Tom

Tom was a partner in an IT company, until, in his late thirties, he became ill, in a way similar to, but not as severe as, my own. No longer able to function in modern office environments—although never, luckily, affected by daylight itself—he has had to find another, home-based life.

His partners in the company buy him out and he decides to use some of the money to build an eco-house for himself, his wife and three children. It will be extremely energy-efficient, and its running costs will be exceptionally low.

I hear about the progress of the house. "The difficult thing," says Tom, "is making the whole place properly airtight, so that you retain the maximum amount of heat. I'm trying to get hold of special seals for the edges of the windows, and for the joins between the walls and the floor."

"If it's completely airtight," I ask, "what about ventilation?"

"There's a single air inlet with a small electric pump. In the summer you can cool the air coming in and in winter you can heat it, if you need to, but it's amazing how much heat human bodies generate, if you keep it in and don't let it escape."

"If the pump broke, would you suffocate?" I ask with interest, thinking of a possible plot for an eco-whodunnit.

"It would take five to six days," says Tom, who always works things like this out. "So you'd probably start to notice before you finally expired. I've installed carbon dioxide monitors, just in case."

Most of the windows in the house face south, to maximise solar gain. A system of blinds prevents overheating. Shade creepers grow up over the porch in summer, and die back in winter, when sunlight is scarce. I have never seen the house, but I have an image of it in my mind as a live thing, a reptile basking in the sun, sucking into its belly every life-giving ray.

Tom is not a fan of conventional wisdom. If he wants to know about something, he researches it himself. He rigs up a computer in an old barn, so that the image that would appear on the monitor is projected on a large scale on to a white wall, and he can sit at a keyboard far enough away from it to avoid discomfort. He thinks the Internet will result in social change on a scale that has scarcely yet been imagined, bringing people together so they can slip out from under the grasp of institutions and governments. People will manage their health without doctors, teach themselves things without schools, share and analyse data to find patterns that would never emerge in traditional scientific trials.

I am stimulated by these new ideas, exhilarated by Tom's optimistic view of the future, encouraged by the chance it gives for people written off by the system to work out their own salvation. But I'm not completely convinced. I mistrust anything that claims to transcend, once and for all, human nature, history and power relations, and offer unmixed liberation. "Don't you think,"

I ask him, "that all this cyber-utopianism, or whatever, could become—well, a bit ideological?"

He doesn't, really. He simply tells me about yet more startling developments in computing and on the Web, and also about what futurologists think will happen next, as computers become smaller and smaller and more and more powerful. Eventually a person will be able to download their entire consciousness, and become an eternal, inorganic intelligence, removing the need for a body, and all the messy fallibility of flesh.

Mother

My mother is coming to visit.

The first sign is the sound of a taxi drawing up. Then there is a banging of car doors, a rustle of bags and a loud cheerful voice in the street outside.

There is more banging and stomping as she unlocks the front door and comes inside.

"Hello-o?" she calls. "Now stay in the black, don't get overexposed."

I come downstairs. In the hall, my mother is divesting herself of a black metallic walking stick, a backpack, a shoulder bag, a carrier bag, a purple coat and a turquoise hat and scarf.

"I've brought various things," she says, delving into her bags. "I went into Sainsbury's opposite the station and bought you some yellow chrysanthemums. You ought to be able to see those in the gloom." She comes into the living room and gives a yell as she walks into the coffee table. (In the dim light, visitors entering from the bright world outside go temporarily blind.)

"I'll just stand here and give my eyes time to adjust," my mother says, handing me a lumpy package. She has brought some raw beets, which she is going to make into borscht for lunch. (Raw beets, strangely, are a metropolitan luxury, very difficult to get hold of in my part of Hampshire.) She has also brought a new mug with a nice strawberry pattern, and some posh jam as a present for Pete, who is a connoisseur of conserves.

My mother sits on the tall chair in the kitchen, chopping up beetroot, while I make cups of tea. She holds forth on:

1. Something outrageous that the government is doing (her indignation is fresh, as she bought a paper to read on the train).

2. Problems she is having with the venue for the music course that she runs twice a year. Many of her punters are past their first youth, but the well-known boarding school she hires has once again assigned them rooms with bunk-beds.

3. My brother, who is too amenable, and can't say no to anyone, which means he takes on too many musical commitments and doesn't get enough exercise.

While the soup cooks, we go upstairs into the black to talk and play games.

After lunch my mother sits down at the piano, and the noise and movement, the bumps and crashes and exclamations, simply fall away, as if a live electric cable has, by connecting to the keyboard, earthed itself; she plays with lucid musical intelligence, serenity and joy. The music comes up through the floor of my dark room, filling it with rippling sound. With human company attached, I can listen, and not be overwhelmed.

When I was growing up, our weekly piano lesson periodically descended into sulking and rage as I tried to master some new aspect of technique. For a while, there was an enterprise known as the "Family Newspaper," written by all family members on large blank sheets of newsprint with felt-tip pens. "Anna is still struggling with the scale of F major," my mother reported in one of her news columns. I was indignant. An entry appeared in the next edition in irregular purple letters: "Mummy is still struggling with the Brahms–Handel variations," it read, referring to a large and virtuoso concert piece.

In my mother I see the source of parts of myself, and also elements so alien that they leave me mystified. Yet my mother is the person to whom I say things about my situation that I say to no one else.

She tells me that another of my cousins has had a baby.

"What is that to me?" I ask. "I don't want to know things that remind me that I am a failure."

She tells me of an acquaintance who has been rushed to hospital, because he was coughing up blood.

"At least he can go to hospital," I say.

My mother says she has spoken to her friend Eleanor,

who has had psychiatric problems for years, and now lives alone, depressed, and hardly ever goes out.

"Can she see the sky outside her window?" I ask. "Can she open her front door and walk along her street? Can she turn on the telly whenever she wants to and watch it for as long as she likes? Then she should bow down and kiss the ground in gratitude."

"I have tried to tell her about you," says my mother.

I would not speak like this to Pete or to my friends, and do so to my mother only rarely. Told of others' joys or misfortunes, I usually respond with friendly interest or appropriate concern. If there is a small dark movement of the heart, it is suppressed, and I find I soon feel, sincerely, what I am saying.

But with my mother I become a child again. "It's not fair," I yell, in more sophisticated language, and my desperate, incontinent jealousy floods out, hot and foul and unconstrained.

What will I do, what will I do, when the time comes, that must inevitably come, and my feisty, bustling mother is dead?

Games to Play in the Dark 3: Mind Mastermind

This is a game for two players. It requires a high degree of logic, concentration and memory, providing an aerobics class for the neural networks.

Each player thinks of a four-letter word, of the polite kind. They take it in turns to attempt to guess each other's word. For every word they ask, the other player gives them a score from 0 to 3 representing the number of letters in the correct positions.

The first to guess the other's word correctly wins.

You have to remember your word. You have to remember the words you've asked. You have to remember the scores you got for them.

Then you apply logic, probability and low cunning to run the other person's word to earth before your own cover is blown. Between two experienced players the game has the beauty and ruthlessness of single combat.

I dream of four-letter words. I search my mind for the most difficult and unusual, listen for them as I absorb my talking books. I fall in love with words like ECRU and HYMN and GNAW; with AWRY, with CHIC and with BULB. I start a small mental stash of the most fiendish in preparation for future competitions with my mother, who is my most frequent and fearsome opponent. My mother is notorious among her friends and relations for being extremely able and competitive at all sorts of games. I can beat her, but I need all my wits about me, and when I manage it, my mother, desensitised to victory, will exclaim, "You always win!"

One day, a game goes like this:

Mother: BELT.
Me: None. PATE.
Mother: None. MUTE.
Me: None. MOOR.
Mother: None. NOSY.
Me: None. SUET.

Mother: None. SHIP.

Me: None. CRAW.

Mother: None. DAMN. That's my go, not a comment, by the way.

Me: None. VEIL.

Mother: How would you be spelling that?

Me: V . . . E . . . I . . . L, as in veil and unveil.

Mother: None. EVER.

Me: None.

Mother: Hmm. I seem to be getting nowhere fast.

Me: Well, I'm not getting anywhere either. Let's see, I haven't tried a Y at the end yet. ALLY.

Mother: None. INTO.

Me: None.

Mother: This must be a very unusual word, to have hit no letters at all.

Me: It isn't, particularly. Is yours?

Mother: I wouldn't say so.

Me: ECHO.

Mother: That's a nice word. None. Perhaps I ought to try some unusual letters. LYNX.

Me: None. LYNX to you.

Mother: None. BUZZ.

Me: None. UGLI with an I—it's a kind of fruit, I think.

Mother: I know what an UGLI is, thank you. None. GREW.

Me: None. ISLE, as in I . . . S . . . L . . . E.

Mother: Hmm, silent letters, eh? None.

Me: Are you sure I've heard of this word?

Mother:	Of course you have. Have I heard of yours?
Me:	Yes—it's a perfectly normal word.
Mother:	(Getting desperate) Goodness, I don't know—perhaps the vowels are in different places. What about OBOE?
Me:	None. (Equally desperate) WHAM.
Mother:	None.
Me:	This is bonkers. Are you sure you haven't given me false information?
Mother:	I don't think so. What about you? TAXI.
Me:	No, I haven't. TAXI has none.

What has happened, of course, is that we have given each other the same word HIGH, and, both being devilishly clever and devious, have avoided asking words with Is and Hs in the relevant places, in order not to give the other person ideas.

Finally, finally, somebody says FISH, and gets two points. The Mexican stand-off is over and, very quickly, all is revealed.

People

Other people visit me, from time to time. Mostly they are people I am sure of, people who will see the girl through the darkness, who will not be fazed by the strangeness of the situation, not be so shocked and flabbergasted that they become distressing companions.

A person called Alicia comes, but only once. "I don't

know how you cope, I couldn't," she says, almost accusingly, over and over again. I wonder what I am expected to do: to scream the whole day long, perhaps, or run down the street in the midday sun in some futile show of defiance and then burn for weeks. Or does my visitor mean, but cannot bring herself to say, that in her view this is a life not worth living, that I should end it, and not embarrass people by dragging my pitiful scrap of existence on through the months and the years?

But for the most part, people—of the right kind—are good. For them I put on my corset of cheerfulness, a solid serviceable garment. It holds in the bulgings and oozings of emotion, and soon I find they are, temporarily, stilled.

People make me tidy up my psyche, as one might order the magazines on the coffee table before a visitor arrives, and afterwards, for a while, they will stay that way, before entropy reasserts its hold.

People remind me of my true shape, the particular bent of my mind, the curve of my wit; that I have substance, though I move wraithlike among shadows, that the years before the darkness laid down rich sediment which has not been washed away.

But there are not enough people. In fairness, I have not made it easy, for them or for myself. Moving to Itchingford from London when I did, I placed geographical, economic and psychological barriers between us, as well as the more subtle ones of divergence of experience, of loss of common ground. To visit me without a car, they must take one or two trains, at least, and then, from the railway station, a twenty-minute cab ride, or a highly circuitous bus. The ones who visit with a car must drive along the M25 and down the M3, length of journey variable, depending on the traffic. In Itchingford itself, the time between my coming and the second disaster has not been long enough, and I have not been well enough, to make new friends, at least of the degree of intimacy required to invite comfortably into tragedy.

Pete, with his own friends, sticks to generalities about our situation, and is vague about the particulars. Constitutionally self-contained and reticent on private matters, he does not, in any context, easily ask for help.

Alex comes to visit, the person for whom I arranged "Little Donkey" in happier times. She says, "I think you're amazing, you cope so well. You are such a strong woman."

That is the sort of thing I like, being only human, after all.

Jonathan, my once-close friend, does not come. He recovers, at least partially, from the bombing, and gets a high-powered job near his home on the far side of the capital, to which he can commute by car. "I must come and visit you," he says, once or twice. It does not happen; soon phone calls also cease.

He was the person, more than any other, with whom I shared my London life. For eight years we would meet after work to go to a play in Shaftesbury Avenue, a concert at the Southbank, or a film at the NFT—all within walking distance of our office—or we would have a meal at our favourite Turkish restaurant, where I would eat too many olives and too much hummus, and give myself indigestion.

Friendship plants itself as a small unobtrusive seed; over time, it grows thick roots that wrap around your heart. When a love affair ends, the tree is torn out quickly, the operation painful but clean. Friendship withers quietly, there is always hope of revival. Only after time has passed do you recognise that it is dead, and you are left, for years afterwards, pulling dry brown fibres from your chest.

MY VISITORS CAN never find the door. They lose their sense of direction completely, and try to get out of the wardrobe, or through the mirror. "Hold still a minute," I say, to stop them blundering about and banging into things. I move quickly, place my hand unerringly on the door handle, and release my confused visitor, who has been fluttering like a bird.

Knitting

I am always trying to think of new things to do in the dark. Hungry for stuff to stuff the empty black hours, my mind ploughs up and down the fields of my experience, turning over the soil of all I've ever done, in case some nugget should rise to the surface, and could be put to use.

I have a memory of doing something with my hands,

something repetitious yet satisfying; something I had to look at to start with to get right, but that after a while I could carry on subconsciously. I remember twisting wool around two needle points, slipping one downwards just enough, allowing one loop to slide over the other, to catch and hold.

I was never good at crafty things when young, being neither meticulous nor neat, but I was definitely better at knitting than anything else. I had even, over two years, painstakingly completed a stripy jumper. Large, bulky and indubitably home-made, it came to a sad end in a charity shop; over the period of its making, I had become an excruciatingly self-conscious sixteen-year-old, and could not bring myself to wear it.

However, I remember the grim satisfaction of generating row after row; there was always visible reward for application in terms of inches produced, clear woolly proof of virtue.

Could this perhaps be just the thing to justify my useless life? I mention my idea to my friend Pam, who is an enthusiastic producer of garments for nephews and nieces. She turns up with a pair of large needles and a bag of thick bright turquoise wool, and gives me a refresher course in the gloom downstairs, nipping into the light of the kitchen to demonstrate the finer points.

The plan is that I am going to knit a scarf, straight up and down, no complicated shaping, in knit two, purl two rib.

I sit on the floor of my room, cross-legged, leaning my back against the side of the bed. To start with I think I can tell the difference between a stitch that has been knitted in the previous row, and therefore wants to be purled (to maintain the ribbed effect), and a stitch that has been purled, and therefore wants to be knitted— partly by feel, and partly by keeping rigorous count in my head. My first few inches, taken downstairs to be examined, have worked well.

But gradually I get more and more confused. I become convinced that a particular sensation of woollen loops under my fingers means I must knit the next stitch rather than purl it, and I proceed for a few rows on that assumption. Then the texture starts to feel different, and I lose my nerve, and try another policy. I count my stitches—but then I find I have an odd and not an even number.

Something has gone very wrong.

I leave my darkness and examine what I have produced. For a band measuring about a couple of inches, the neat ribbed stripes have gone haywire, all bobbly and uneven, as though affected by some lichenous growth.

Stupidly, I do not rip it out. Instead, I say to myself, "Oh well, it doesn't have to be perfect; this is just my practice scarf." And I correct my approach, and concentrate hard, and over the next couple of days (I don't do it all the time) I produce another few inches of rib.

And then I look at it again, with the horrible messed-up band, and begin to wonder: who will wear this scarf anyway, why am I doing this at all, what is it for, when a better one could easily be bought? And I come to a halt, caught between two contradictory impulses—not wanting to continue, when the article will have such a flaw, but entirely unable to contemplate unravelling the rows which represent so many hours of slow and solitary toil. And it could so easily go wrong, again.

My fingers falter, the needles drop from my hands. I roll up and impale the ball of wool, stow the knitting in its plastic bag, and reach it on to the top of the wardrobe, so that it is well out of the way, even in the darkness. It has become a tangled web of wool and emotion, and working out what to do about it is currently beyond my powers.

Dream 3

I have one recurring dream. In the dream, I wake in the night. There has been an earthquake, or a violent storm. It has torn a huge jagged hole in the wall that runs along the side of my bed. The bed is tilted at a crazy angle, the head end canted downwards, sticking through the hole and into the world outside. Rain is falling on my face, wetting my pillow and my sheets; a night breeze caresses my hair and swirls the raindrops against my skin.

Then I jolt awake for real. Good God, I think, what on earth am I doing? There's a hole in the side of my bedroom, and I'm just lying here, exposing my skin to the light in the street outside. I must be mad. I reach my hand out to measure the breach in my wall—and my palm finds nothing but unbroken painted plaster, smooth and bland and dry.

I slam my hand against the wall. I roll my body again

and again, smashing my bones against its cool, implacable façade.

How did I end like this? I pick over the months that led up to my final boxing-in, attempting to impose order on a sequence of events that, lived through, passed in a horrific accelerating blur.

Now I can recollect them in tranquillity; I have the time.

Oh I have the time, indeed.

April 2006

I lie on a bed wrapped in thick black felt from head to foot, one portion of my upper arm exposed, while a huge angled lamp, warm like a miniature sun, plays different frequencies of light upon my naked skin.

"It's my face that reacts," I say to the technician, after she has unwrapped me. "Not the rest of me, thank goodness."

"Oh, everyone has light testing," she replies. "Just to eliminate things. It's routine."

She gets me to sit upright, this time with my back exposed, and draws a grid on it with black felt-tip pen. She fires a particular frequency into each square using a smaller, more focused device. I can see what is happening in a mirror—there is green light and blue light and orange light and red light.

"It's my face," I say again, but this does not seem to be important at this stage.

"You can discuss your results with the consultant tomorrow," says the technician.

I get dressed, put on my hat, and mask up for the journey home.

DR. OCELOT IS a very typical consultant. He is tall and well-made, with regular features and piercing eyes. He has thick, sleek, executive hair, distinguished silver in colour. He has an obsequious student with him in his consulting room, short, pudgy and asymmetrical, but who clearly hopes one day to gleam and glare like his mentor.

"According to your results," drawls Dr. Ocelot, flipping through papers on his desk, "you don't have lupus, porphyria or XP, which are the usual causes of light sensitivity. Will you describe again what the problem seems to be?"

I go through what has happened to my face, how it first reacted to computer screens, went on to fluorescent lights, and is now giving me trouble with daylight. I demonstrate my hat and mask.

"And what exactly are the symptoms you experience?"

I explain about the burning and indicate the red patches.

"And what precisely do you mean by burning?"

I am starting to lose patience. Why is the default setting of doctors always disbelief? Do they really think I've jumped through hoops to get here merely because of some minor discomfort? Or that I've travelled to the clinic in my outlandish gear as some sort of exhibition-ist fashion statement? Even the student is practising his sceptical expression, modelling himself upon the master.

I say, "It is like someone is holding a blowtorch in front of my face."

That gets them. There is an interval of shocked silence; the image seems to have punched through the professional barrier between us, to have made them feel what I am feeling, if only for a moment.

Dr. Ocelot leans back in his chair, steepling his fingers and gazing at the ceiling. "We do occasionally come across cases like this," he acknowledges. "The diagnosis is light- and computer-exacerbated seborrhoeic dermatitis. It is not clear what causes it. I am going to prescribe beta blockers to reduce blood flow, steroid creams and an antifungal wash. Come back and see us in six to eight weeks. You won't be seeing me, though. I am going to take up a post in the USA. You will be in the care of my colleague, Dr. Scrivener, whom I think you met briefly yesterday."

I did. Dr. Scrivener is much younger, slim and neat with thinning hair. He has a gentle pink-and-white complexion and an air of genuine benevolence and concern.

I avoid smiling only by forcibly holding down the corners of my mouth.

Later, I leave the hospital pharmacy, weighed down with pills and unguents in several paper bags.

May 2006

I wash with the antifungal wash. I apply the steroid creams. I take the pills. My face experiences some relief. It becomes less rough and raw, the reactions are dampened down, the redness fades away.

After a few days, I start to notice a slight puffy sensation in my arms and legs—it feels like a mild allergic reaction. I think nothing of it—my face is improving, and that's the main thing. I carry on applying the stuff to my skin.

Early May: I am on a train into London, to attend my piano teaching course.

I am in a window seat, my bare forearm stretched out on the table in front of me, palm upward. It is bare because the day is unexpectedly warm and sunny, a sudden foretaste of summer, and I'm wearing a top with sleeves that only come down as far as the elbow.

And I feel a sort of roughed-up sensation on my arm, as though someone is rubbing it with sandpaper. And I peer at my flesh, but can see nothing unusual. And it still feels odd, when I get home that night.

I will always remember that arm—pale and creamy smooth, emerging from a turquoise cotton sleeve on to the grey Formica table top, all the colours vivid in the light streaming through the train window; and that odd rough sensation, the first gentle touch from the tentacles of hell.

A few days later I am in the passenger seat of the car Pete is driving. It is nearly noon on a sunny day; the sun slants down through the windscreen. I am wearing trousers—a thin sort of cord. I notice a rough, burning feeling on the tops of my thighs. It lasts for the rest of the day.

Middle of May: I am on my evening run. A brilliant deep blue empty sky, warm grey tarmac under my feet, low golden rays that make the boring brickwork of the boxy houses blaze, mixed scents of white blossoms.

Suddenly I feel strangely hot all over, and break into a clammy sweat. I stop and stand on the pavement, disconcerted. It is as if something inside me is trying to get out through my skin, not just in one place, but everywhere. I turn and run for home by the shortest route. That night, I tingle all over for hours, and then go deathly cold.

I still do not make the connection. I am focused on my face: that is where light affects me, surely not elsewhere, and my face has got much better. And on the rest of me, unlike my face, there is nothing to see—no redness, no roughness; my covering is intact. It must be some sort of allergy, I conclude, and apply myself to working out what I have eaten, or what I have inhaled, or what I have put on my skin. I go to the GP and am given a referral to an allergy clinic several weeks hence. I become fixated on chlorine in the bathwater when I have a bath one Sunday morning, a decadent luxurious soak in a sun-filled bathroom, and burn afterwards, for hours.

I miss the final sessions of my piano course—feeling too weird, too often, to risk the trips up to town. The organisers say they will still let me qualify, if I send a tape of my performance of the sonata I've been analysing, and write an in-depth essay on the use of twentieth-century piano music for teaching beginner and intermediate students, which I undertake to do.

Towards the end of May, Pete goes away to a conference. Before he leaves, he prints out from the computer the wedding invitations we have designed, plus a set of address labels, and information sheets for the guests. It is my job, in his absence, to get everything sent out.

So one day after lunch, I take all the mats off the dining table next to the south-facing French windows, and wipe it clean of sticky food. I bring down the different piles from the computer room upstairs, lay them out before me, and set to work. First, I stick labels on to the pile of envelopes. Then, taking each envelope in turn, I write on to an invitation the relevant names, fold up a sheet of information, and slip both inside.

As I do it, my skin starts to prickle and burn.

Reach—write—fold.

Reach—write—fold.

Burn.

Neat white rectangles are building up around me, covering one end of the table, falling on to the chairs, spreading across the carpet like stepping stones.

Reach—write—fold.

Burn.

And I am overwhelmed by the hope and hopelessness of what I am doing, by the impossible, unbearable contrast between the joyful invitation with which I fill each envelope and the random and fathomless thing rampaging through my skin, ever more frequent, ever more painful, that is lengthening, lengthening, lengthening the odds that this wedding will ever take place.

I crumple over the table, my face pressed into my hands, and cry harder than I have ever cried, the spasms so intense that I twist from my chair and tumble to the floor, shrieking and writhing among the envelopes, streaking them with tears. It is as if I am being torn in two down my centre line; I have never experienced such an intense bifurcation of soul.

Crying brings its own relief. Some sort of chemical is released, I have heard, that normalises the mood, even as the situation itself remains unchanged; a wise self-limiting mechanism, for which, doubtless, we have evolution to thank.

I push myself to a sitting position and shove my messy hair out of my face. I look at the piles on the table, and estimate that my task is about half-complete. If I finish it, and get rid of it, I won't have to think about it again.

Wearily I climb back into my seat. "Don't feel," I instruct myself. What is this, after all, but stuffing envelopes, a routine administrative task? In my mind's eye, I take a splinter of ice, and I plunge it into my heart.

A FEW DAYS later, I am in the north-facing spare room, sprawled on the bed barefoot, reading, when finally the sun itself has mercy on me. It is setting where it only does in summer, to the north-west of the house. Slowly it moves down the sky, slipping quietly into position, lining itself up with my window, carefully preparing its strike.

The rays shoot into the room with the power and intensity of a laser, and I feel my feet ignite. Seconds later, in my mind, comes hideous illumination, a parody of St. Paul's blinding light. Here, at last, is the truth, stark and unarguable, with no space left for doubt. I have my cause and my effect; other possibilities burn away, like flesh on a heretic's bones.

For a while I lie without moving, held under the claw of the sun. The room is bathed in peachy golden light, the bedclothes and the bookshelves strangely beautiful. I make no attempt to shield myself; I need to feel the burning of my feet, to keep on feeling it, to understand in every part of me that this is real, to know the world will not unwind itself and take a different, more convenient path.

I hear footsteps mount the stairs. "Pete," I call out, my voice cracking in my throat.

"You OK, darling?" he asks, coming in and sitting on the bed.

I throw myself on to him and bury my face in his chest. "I know what it is," I say. "I've worked it out. Oh Pete—it's the light."

"You mean—on the rest of you?"

"Yes. I don't know what's happened, but somehow, things have reversed themselves. My face has got better—but the rest of me—the sensitivity—it's gone all over. Oh Pete, what am I going to do?"

"My dear," he says, hugging me tightly to him, "my poor dear." Then, after a while: "Well, at least we know

now. That has to be a step forward. Would it be an idea to close these curtains?"

I snort with damp laughter. "Er . . . yes, it probably would."

He draws a veil across the setting sun, which drops luxuriously into a foamy pink bath of cloud, its work complete.

Eclipse

Once, I witnessed a total solar eclipse. It was the one that took place on 11 August 1999, and it was visible across parts of south-west England and northern France, if the sky was not cloudy at the critical point.

I had a friend with a connection to the Royal Astronomical Society. The Society organised a special trip to watch the eclipse in the Channel Islands, open to members, families and hangers-on.

Four of us hung on. We flew to Guernsey and spent three nights in a hotel beneath the airport flight path; the roar of planes taking off and landing started in the early hours and continued until late at night.

On the morning of the day itself, we rose well before dawn and caught a bus to the port, where a huge white ship, specially chartered, loomed above the dock. Many astronomers were already on board, carrying impressive collections of telescopic and photographic equipment. Children ran about the decks in a state of high excitement. The ship nosed out into a choppy sea to cross to the island of Alderney, which lies on its own about twenty miles north-east of Guernsey, not far away from France.

At the start of the voyage the sky was cloudless blue, and the spirits of the astronomers high. When we arrived at Alderney, however, a pall of grey had settled over the island, and the main topic of conversation was the prospects for it lifting before 10:12 a.m., the time of first contact, when the moon's disc first touches the edge of the sun.

Buses were waiting for us on the quay. For a while, a large Womble danced ahead of us along the road, waving its arms in a cheerful manner, a traditional way, perhaps, of welcoming visitors to a place with fewer obvious attractions than the other Channel Islands, but which was the home of Elizabeth Beresford, who wrote the Womble books.

The buses deposited us at a ruined fort, a massive circle of jagged stone walls perched on cliffs above the sea. According to the notice boards it was used by the Germans when the islands were under occupation in the Second World War. The place had a strange bleak atmosphere, a sort of resistance to questioning. The flat expanse of ground within the walls was covered thickly with many kinds of weeds.

The astronomers swarmed over the fort, finding good places to set up, an occupying army bearing black, long-barrelled equipment, which they carefully angled heavenwards on spindly sets of legs.

The high grey cloud began to mottle and shift, becoming less uniform.

Then the eclipse was upon us, and the moon began to nibble at the edge of the sun.

More serendipitous gaps appeared in the messy spider's web of cloud, revealing the protagonists in plain view. Through my eclipse glasses I saw the small black fingermark, the almost imperceptible imperfection, that was the beginning.

Then, as the moon slid further over the disc of the sun, the fort was illuminated by a melancholy golden light, as though at eleven o'clock in the morning evening had come, with the sun high overhead.

I looked through my glasses again, and watched a black lid slipping remorselessly over a jar of fire. Then, as the sky darkened, I stood precariously balanced on a flat slab of stone, and watched the moon's shadow zoom towards us over the sea.

I will never forget the speed, the terrible speed of that approach. My breath stopped in my throat, as though the shadow itself sucked away the air as it dashed across the waves. We were being given a glimpse of the true speed of the rotation of the earth, of that perpetual, massive, onward roll going on beneath our feet. Soon there remained only one last bulge of radiance at the side of the sun, and a faint outline of the rest, the stage known as the "diamond ring." Finally even that last bubble of light was extinguished. Night fell.

And then, two minutes later—the jar was slowly opened again. Once more, the gem now placed on the opposite side, there was a diamond ring, and then the mysterious, unearthly golden glow, this time signifying a resurrected not a dying sun. By lunchtime, all had returned to normality, leaving a mood of euphoria that filled the fort. Everyone smiled at each other, because we knew that we had shared a memorable thing: for an infinitesimal fragment of cosmic time, we had put one finger on the pulse of the universe, and felt its beat.

June 2006

In the weeks that follow the spare-room revelation, darkness rushes towards me, as the shadow of the moon rushed over the sea.

Outside the house I no longer leave, summer opens its jaws wider each day, revealing more of its teeth. With each rotation of the earth, the sun bounces up earlier in the morning, arcs higher, lingers longer around the shrinking pool of night. I have to keep the curtains closed, at first only halfway, then fully; at first only to keep out direct rays, then against the mere glare of the day, while the sun itself is busy round another part of the house.

Pete searches the Internet on my behalf. He finds a support group for people living with light sensitivity— part of the charity Lupus UK, but including members whose light sensitivity arises from some other source.

The name of the group is Eclipse.

There is a list on their website of products that might prove useful. We throw money at the problem—it seems rational to try everything.

A man comes with a squeegee, a spray gun and a

large roll of clear film. He spends a morning filming most of the windows of the house. The film stops the transmission of UV light, the highest and most damaging frequency.

I order UV-protective clothing from a specialist company. It is made of densely knitted nylon and Lycra, slightly stretchy, not very aesthetic. I have a hooded top and loose trousers in pale blue, plus grey socks; I feel like an extra from a science-fiction film.

For a few days, inside my new packaging, I have some relief. I seem to have found a plateau of stability where, if I live within certain parameters, my skin will not burn. I relax, even become cheerful, joking about my new suit.

But the stability is an illusion, the sensitivity soon on the march once more.

The experience is like falling over a cliff in slow motion. After each lurch downwards I think I've found a toehold, or a shrub to grasp to break my fall. I'm sure, each time, I must have reached a stable place, a place where, despite my undignified position, I can at least not slip further, can start to consider the options for climbing back to the top.

The ledge crumbles, the shrub rips from the cliff face, every, every time.

I lose myself in thick absorbent books. On Pete's bookshelves I find the complete works of Jane Austen in a single volume, leather-bound in red. I start *Sense and Sensibility* sitting at a table in the living room with the curtain slightly open, but my posture becomes increasingly bizarre. After a few days I am crouched on the floor, screened by a wall and an armchair, hunched over to catch the faintest flicker of print.

A few days later, Pete comes in from the local summer fete, carrying a big bag of books. He had been helping as usual on the second-hand book stall and has not been able to resist purchasing some of its wares. He finds me cross-legged on the sofa, in a curtained room, most of my body under a thick black padded anorak, wrapped around like a blanket, and I am reading *Persuasion*, by the indirect light that comes through the kitchen door.

"This seems to work," I say to him, indicating the anorak, and I even smile. "Let's see what you got."

I think he is appalled, but he does not let it show. We look at the books he has bought. I am burying my head in alternative realities, forcing it out of my own.

SOME TIME IN the middle of all this is my follow-up appointment at the hospital. The idea that I could leave the house, let alone get to London, is laughable. I phone the photobiology clinic and explain my situation to the medical secretary. "OK, I'll cancel that for you," she says. "Give us a ring when you're feeling better."

I am not in a fit state fully to appreciate the irony of that response.

Vanishing Point

People continue to search online for something—anything—that could help. Parcels of A4 printouts arrive for me in the post from friends of mine, of Pete's, and of my mother's, to whom, in desperation, she has poured out my story. There is a lot of information about photosensitivity, but nothing about photosensitivity as severe and unusual as mine.

Then, suddenly, from two directions, there is news: a scientific paper describing a case like mine in Sweden, and, via another support group, a contact for a real live person, living in the UK.

Somebody else like me.

His name is Jake and he lives in Manchester. He is in his thirties. He is excruciatingly sensitive to all forms of light.

I speak to his partner on the phone. "What he has found," she says, "is that if he spends time in a completely blacked-out room, his skin builds up a bit of resilience, and he can tolerate some limited light, for a while, when he comes out."

As soon as she says it, it makes sense to me. Already, in a confused way, I have been groping towards a similar conclusion. Scoured by the sun each day from 4 a.m., I know that normal curtains are no longer an effective bar. Now I have a clear picture of what I need, and, in anticipation, my skin breathes a sigh of relief. I start to yearn for the dark, I want it now, I do not want to wait. A dying traveller in a desert strains to glimpse the saving glint of water; I long for the space before my eyes to void itself of every hint of light.

It is not easily achieved. Materials and fixings must be obtained, and even after they are installed, I have to resort to foil.

When I have finished, I lie exhausted on the bed. I feel as though I have completed a long and arduous operation involving the amputation of one of my own limbs. In fact I have merely hacked away the light from my life, but it has been a procedure equally grisly, complex, necessary, traumatic and appalling. Around me in the darkness the carpet, the walls, the curtains and the bookshelves swim with invisible gore.

I am beyond thinking. I have reached my vanishing point.

AFTER A WHILE I come round, to find strange sounds emanating from the room below. There is jeering and yelling, and the rise—rise—rise—and fall of commentary. Pete's voice suddenly exclaims, "Oh! . . . ah . . ." then "YESSS!"

It is the World Cup of 2006, and somebody has just scored a goal.

Autonomy

There were many things I wanted to be different, in the life before. I wanted to be more organised so that I left work on time, and could undertake some regular evening activities. I wanted to be more confident when giving presentations, and address my audience in a louder voice. I wanted to get on better with a certain friend of Pete's, whom he esteemed highly, but I found smug and cold.

To each of these things I could hope to apply time, effort and willpower, and expect to achieve, if not total transformation, at least a degree of improvement.

With casual brutality, illness reminds us of the limits of human will. At each stage of my decline, getting the first inklings of the next phase of horror, I would say to myself, repeatedly, "I will not let this happen." And it happened, nonetheless. In my body, something was afoot; there had been treachery within the citadel. Quietly an alien force crept in, overwhelming the loyal defenders, taking and holding the positions of strength. My will is left to roam impotently in one small tower, surveying its occupied domain.

How did I end like this? If I had known more, at each stage, of the possibility of the next—oh, I would have exercised all my prudence and efficiency, all my ingenuity, intelligence and cunning in the service simply of preserving what I had. But at each stage, I was an oddity, never to be warned, merely to be funnelled to the next layer of specialists, through an ever-narrowing conduit, until I reached this vanishing point.

Did I reach it via a chain of contingent trivial choices, where at each stage, had I acted slightly differently, the outcome would have been altered? Or was it written in my stars, or in my genes, or in my soul, so that I would have reached it regardless, in any case, through the iron determination of fate? I am not sure which metaphysical system is the more terrifying, or terrible.

This is why I find the novels of Thomas Hardy particularly harrowing as companions in the dark. I have to ration my exposure, and sometimes simply give them up. He is the novelist par excellence of the small thing with the huge consequences, of the everyday mischance that leads to tragedy, of the almost invisible membrane that divides success and failure, thin as the letter that slides beneath the carpet when Tess slips it under Angel's door.

Correspondence 1

"We should do something about the wedding," says Pete, "to take the pressure off."

What? Oh yes—the wedding. The struggle for survival over the last few weeks has absorbed so much of my brain that I have nearly forgotten about it. But actually making the decision to cancel—blindingly, obviously necessary as it is—still hurts, the final amputation of a putrefied dream.

More envelope stuffing—this time, only one sheet in each. Pete does most of it. I stuff what I can.

14 July 2006

. . . Over the last few weeks Anna's health has deteriorated badly and she has become extremely sensitive to light. So, very reluctantly, we have decided to postpone our wedding. Thank you for all your donations to our charities. Our apologies go to everyone who has already booked travel or accommodation for

9 September. We still hope to have a wedding some time in the future and will hope to see you there . . .

Correspondence 2

. . . When I first saw Dr. Ocelot in April, only the patches of dermatitis on my face were photosensitive. Now it appears that the whole of my body is reacting . . .

What provision is made for people who are too ill to attend the London clinic? I am not sure how to proceed and would welcome some assistance . . .

. . . I am sorry to hear that things have got so much worse with your health. This is a very difficult situation and I am sorry that you find yourself in this situation. When patients are unable to come to see us for these reasons, then the local doctors take up their role again . . .

. . . Thank you for phoning last Thursday. You explained that while 90 per cent of photosensitivity cases can now be linked to a specific clinical condition, 10 per cent remain which cannot be, in the present state of knowledge . . .

I said that I would send you a paper my fiancé

found on the Internet which describes a case of photosensitivity which exactly matches what has happened to me:

1. Initial symptoms were "screen dermatitis," i.e., redness and burning on the face when using a VDU.

2. Generalised all-over light sensitivity set in after one intense but reasonably short exposure (in my case going for a run earlier than usual on a bright May evening).

3. Symptoms of the generalised light sensitivity (in contrast to the facial "screen dermatitis" symptoms) are a severe burning sensation, but *with no rash or visible sign.*

. . . Are there any aids which one can take for living in the dark? Are there supplements which one should take to make up for lack of sunlight? . . .

. . . Many thanks for the copy of the article. We and other colleagues have certainly seen patients with symptoms like yours and like those of the patient in the article. At the moment the cause of the condition is unknown. It would certainly seem reasonable to ask your GP for some vitamin D supplementation since sunlight does help to produce vitamin D in the

skin, and this would prevent you becoming deficient in vitamin D . . .

I am sorry not to give more specific and helpful advice, but this really reflects the current lack of understanding of the condition . . .

. . . If your condition improves sufficiently to allow travel to London, please do inform us so we can arrange an appointment . . .

. . . We have had to cancel our wedding because of my deteriorated health. As you know when we decided to get married and took out wedding insurance the only part of me affected with light sensitivity was my face. I had no idea at that time that the condition could evolve and spread to the extent that it has . . .

. . . The points you make in terms of the insurance for the wedding are entirely reasonable and . . . I will explain this to the insurance company if they contact me . . .

. . . As far as collecting knowledge and understanding of your condition are concerned things are still at the early observational stage . . .

. . . I am now aware of three other people in England who have developed my form of severe photosensitivity and are living in darkness. There is a real issue of access to services. It would be useful to know what research is being carried out or planned into this particularly disabling form of photosensitivity . . .

. . . If I hear of specific research projects occurring in this area I will keep you posted. Obviously, it is a disease which is particularly difficult in terms of research . . .

. . . The situation I am in seems a bit bonkers in that I am excluded from treatment unless I can become "well" enough to attend your clinic! I would be willing to pay for a private telephone consultation . . .

. . . .

. . . It would be really helpful to talk things through with you—is there any possibility of a telephone appointment?

. . . .

Games to Play in the Dark 4: Word Square

This is a game to play on your own, when you crave violent relief from chaotic, churning thoughts.

Roll out a large white sheet of paper in your mind. Pin it down at each corner, so you cannot see the wriggling underneath. Draw on it a grid, five squares by five. Place letters into the squares on the grid, so that they form five-letter words, both down the columns and across the rows.

It seems simple, but is very, very hard.

Even with multiple substitutions of letters and complete reversals of strategy, virtually all attempts will end in failure, abandonment, or falling asleep. Yet the possibility of success continues to glimmer on the horizon, a goad to further effort. You find yourself developing theories regarding the most productive approach, at times favouring the "vowel consonant vowel consonant vowel" method (and vice versa on the line underneath); at other times always starting in the top left-hand corner with an S, and bunching consonants together around it. You begin to favour words like STRAP, easily flexed in many different directions (STROP, STRAW, SCRAP) to accommodate disastrous impasses reached in other parts of the grid.

S	C	R	A	P
S	R	I	D	E
L	O	V	E	S
I	N	E	P	T
T	E	N	T	S

I did it once.

Physics

In the life before, I held a layman's view of light. I considered it to be a substance much like water: you could bathe in it if you took off your clothes, and when you opened curtains it streamed in. You would always be able to see it with your eyes; if you could not, it was not there.

From such feeble, poetic notions I have been brutally disabused by the physics lesson that has incubated in my skin.

Light is the smiling blue-eyed daughter of a family of ruffians—superficially innocent, but sharing many traits in common with her wilder relations. Gamma rays, X-rays, ultra-violet rays, microwaves and radio waves are the fellow members of her tribe—self-perpetuating electromagnetic disturbances that travel from their point of origin at great speed and across great distances, falling off only gradually in strength. Humans on earth can detect waves from the very edges of the universe, and it is not impossible that other intelligences, in other galaxies, are listening, albeit with several years' delay, to Radio 4.

The speed of all electromagnetic waves is the same. It is a constant, most commonly referred to as the speed of light, around 300,000 km a second in a vacuum. According to the theory of relativity, it is the maximum speed that is possible, in this universe, with this set of physical laws.

Electromagnetic waves each have a particular frequency and wavelength; it is these that give each kind of wave its own peculiar properties, the frequency always decreasing as the wavelength gets longer. Gamma rays have the highest frequency (around 10^{22} cycles per second) and the shortest wavelength (10^{-14} metres). If the human body is exposed to gamma rays, the DNA in its cells is damaged, and cancers will form. X-rays also penetrate the body, but are not harmful in small doses, and can be put to practical use. The wavelengths of microwaves are measurable in centimetres. They are the workhorses of the telecommunications revolution, whizzing between mobile phones, masts, laptops and Wi-Fi transmitters, carrying data as streams of noughts and ones. Radio waves are longer and more languid, their waves measuring tens or hundreds of metres between peaks. They are the frequency of choice for television and broadcasting, snaking across the country bearing collective information and entertainment.

Light sits on the electromagnetic spectrum between X-rays and microwaves, occupying a narrow band. Its wavelengths are measurable in nanometres, one nanometre being one thousand millionths of a metre. It has the unique property among electromagnetic waves of being visible to the human eye. In fact, it stimulates the retina across a rainbow of seven colours, from violet light (with a wavelength of 400 nanometres) to red light (with a wavelength of 760 nanometres). We perceive white light when the different colour wavelengths are all equally present, so that the different colour-sensitive receptors in our eyes are stimulated to the same degree.

The strength of an electromagnetic wave is always 1

divided by the distance from its source. This is a quantity that gradually reduces, but which will never get to zero. These waves do not disappear; they merely become too weak to register on human detection equipment. They pass, to varying degrees, through material barriers, suffer degrees of diminution in strength, and yet, in their essential nature, persist.

This persistence, above all, is what I discovered as I started my journey into the dark. At first I thought that clothes would solve it, that it was a matter of the wearing of long-sleeved, high-necked, long-skirted garments, in opaque material.

But the light—even indoor light—got through.

So I began to wear layers of clothing—lined jackets over long-sleeved T-shirts, full-length double-layered skirts over black leggings and knee-high boots. It was an intriguing, retro, mildly Edwardian look; I found the best fabric for my long skirts was a densely woven silk, and for my fitted jackets, velvet or corduroy.

But it was not enough.

I discovered that fabric protected better if it was not tightly pressed to the layers beneath, so my silk skirts became tiered and full so they did not cling around my legs, and I swapped my leggings for under-trousers, like Victorian pantaloons.

But it was not enough. The light got through. Beneath my complicated finery, I still burned.

Through horrible experiment, I learnt that walls were what I had to wear, that there was no alternative to walls, that walls, from this point on, would be my perpetual outer garment, my solitary fashion statement, my signature look.

Did I give up too soon? I would gladly have worn a burka in the streets of my small town, if there had been any point. I thought sometimes of armour, or the costume of a Dalek. Would such casings have worked? Perhaps they would not have been too heavy and uncomfortable, the neighbours would have grown accustomed to a shiny, ponderous figure clanking among the hedges and parked cars, no teenage gangs would taunt or knock it over, and after the first YouTube sensation the world would let it make its way in peace.

But by the time I contemplated such extremities, I was worn out by pain, astonished by the incredible level of my own sensitivity, terrified of doing anything to increase it. I could no longer afford to be the subject of my own experiments; I slipped between the walls of my dark room with nothing but relief.

Inside my room, I dress every day in a long-sleeved top and velvet jacket, pull on my pantaloons underneath my silk skirt, slip on socks. I find, by now, that even in darkness *I cannot wear less* (because darkness, of course, is not true darkness, is not a total absence of light).

So there I sit, a sumptuous creature, all set to be the heroine of a novel by Sir Walter Scott, or some other Gothic tale, involving dungeons, dark towers, wicked uncles, imperilled innocence and rustling silks.

In the winter, spring and autumn my layers would be practical enough. In the summer, when the temperature climbs towards 86°F and the sun slams down on the roof and thunders against the walls, and the air in the sealed-up room grows inexorably hotter, as if the black room were a clay pot in an oven and I the meat inside, and I cannot open a window to let in the smallest breath of new air, because the light would get in too, and I cannot strip off my finery, even though my body is cooking, because if I unwrap my flesh I will burn, even through the sealed-up windows and the stopped-up door—in the summer, I lie on the floor, inert, in the lowest, coolest part of the room, and I sweat, and I sweat, and I sweat, and the heat builds day on day, as the heatwave goes on, with no sign of a break in the weather (I listen to every forecast), and I know what it is like to be in hell.

In such situations, life simplifies. Psychological niceties melt away; I abandon the luxury of higher, complex emotion. Nothing is important except physical survival, and to that end everything can be sacrificed: dignity, hygiene, self-respect, activity, visitors (who would simply add to the heat and fetidity), the occasional indulgence of tears. Ice becomes my friend—I freeze plastic bottles of water and surround my body with them, as though packing ice around a corpse. Small electric fans push over me the heavy, baking air.

Late in the evening, when the lazy sun has finally slid below the horizon and the sky is the deep blue of summer nights, I risk going downstairs for a while. Pete goes into the hot black room, pulls back the curtains, raises the blinds and opens one window. He wheels in an air-conditioning unit, pokes out of the window its long flexible white hose, plugs it in and switches it on.

The temperature display shows the temperature in the room is 77°F. By the time I come back up, the air conditioning dismantled and the room resealed, that has reduced to 70°F, not a huge improvement, but still blissful, for me.

I hold to one certainty: that the earth beneath me is turning, and the season of heat must pass, and I will have several months in which to forget, before my inferno returns.

Feral

During the heatwave, I spend a lot of time on the floor of my room. At the end of the season, as the heat begins to pass, the capacity to think slowly returns to me. I become once more cognisant of my surroundings, and discover something horrible and strange.

I am lying on a thick mat of hair. It has meshed itself into the fibres of the carpet, and can be removed only with difficulty. I have to scrape at it with my fingernails to loosen even a few tangled strands.

The hair is long, wavy and brown. It is my own.

I am not shedding more than the average—we all lose several hairs each day. I am unusual only in the intensity with which I have inhabited a single space, and my inability to see the cumulative effect.

In the end I take a comb and comb my carpet, tearing up handful after handful. There is enough to knit into a garment, or to build nests for several birds.

All this hair makes me feel feral, as though I am a

monster that lives beyond human norms, a creature of musky smells and night-time habits, a beast who hunts and claws and bites, and tears the throats out of its prey.

The Smell of the World

Oh, the smell of the world, to those who are not in it. When I hover on the threshold between the inside and the out—opening or closing a fanlight, or beside an open door at night—the smell fizzes in my nostrils like champagne.

It is a cocktail of subtle and infinite parts, better than the finest blends of master perfumers, a compound of life and decay, of growth, damp and wildness, of heat, dust, leaves and flowers, tarmac, cars, earth, stone and stars.

My nose quests after it, drawn forwards like the snout of a dog, yearning to suck in the freshness, to hoover it up like cocaine. It is overwhelming, unutterably tantalising. I stagger, intoxicated. Then I turn back to my darkness, and must smell, for a few moments before my nose adjusts, the staleness, the inferiority, the used-up air of my prison.

An Extraordinary Animal

Pete goes to Cornwall for a few days to take photographs of rocks, cliffs and the sea. He returns with an extraordinary animal as a present for me. It is a sheep made of a white silky hairy material, with hooves of golden plush. Its brown glass eyes bear a wonderfully benign expression. It wears a small patterned bow tie. But its most striking features are its exceptionally long and flexible hind legs, which allow it to do the splits, both front-to-back and sideways, with ease. The sheep is designed to keep out draughts by doing the splits across the bottom of doors. Pete has bought it for me as a light excluder for my dark room, to replace the unattractive sausage of yellow and brown checked fabric that somebody found in an attic, and that I have been using up until now.

When I am given the sheep, I am completely overcome. I can't stop laughing, but I am also close to tears. Into my horribly limited life Pete has still found a way to bring wit and joy and silliness. The sheep, even in the most undignified and eye-watering positions, retains its air of benevolent serenity. At first this leads us to name it "Stoic," but the name doesn't stick. In the end it becomes simply "Long-legged Sheep," and it lives splayed across the threshold of my dark room, an unobtrusive, conscientious guardian. Its presence gives rise to a strange phrase, possibly unique to these peculiar circumstances, never requiring articulation by any other human tongues. "Always replace the sheep," I remind my visitors, because it is inevitably shoved out of the way when they come through the door of my room. "No problem," the visitor says, reaching down into the dark and rearranging the hairy, flexible limbs.

Health and Safety

Spontaneous removal of clothes on the living-room floor is a thing of the past. To make love now, Pete and I require Procedures.

First we must wait until nightfall. Then, before he comes into my black room, Pete switches off the lights in the rest of the house, closes curtains, shuts doors, banishes any stray photons that might fall on naked flesh. Then he must find his way to my lair. He has become better at this, less likely to end up in the airing cupboard, or bash into the bookcase as he comes through the door.

I reach out to touch him once he is inside the room. I wriggle past him to lay the sheep along the bottom of the door. Then I wriggle back, stand up with my body against his, and take him in my arms.

Now we can get down to business. "James Bond never had these difficulties," grumbles Pete, as he struggles to grasp the operating principle of an unfamiliar fastening by touch alone.

"Hmm," I say, having unbuttoned him, "I thought I was getting somewhere, but you appear to be wearing a vest."

Once, in the early days, we knocked our heads together so hard that we both saw stars. Pete has ground his elbow into my eye; on another occasion, I punched him on the jaw and his head hit the wall beside the bed. It is a single bed, and we have also fallen out of it, both jointly and severally.

At Pete's place of work, there is a big campaign to eliminate "lost time accidents." Employees are showered with leaflets exhorting them not to run on the stairs, and to look both ways before they cross the road. Pete and I wonder what a risk assessor would make of our activities. Would he ban them outright, perhaps, or insist on the wearing of hard hats? The trick, we have discovered, is to make sure the other person always knows where your head is. So we talk more, or make sounds. This also helps to make up for the absence of facial expressions indicating ecstasy, boredom, delight, etc.

I worry less now about noise; with the window shrouded in layers of blackout, it is unlikely that anyone will be able to hear.

Green Things

Tonight there is a competition at the camera club on the theme of "British Nature." Pete comes into my dark room, and sits on the bed beside me to tell me about it.

"All the people who like taking pictures of insects will come out of the woodwork," he predicts. "There will be lots of close-ups of long-bodied chasers, and that sort of thing."

A long-bodied chaser is a kind of dragonfly. "What are you going to enter?" I ask.

Pete is more into landscape than nature, so he will not have a lot of choice. On his camera he shows me a very fuzzy highly abstract close-up of indeterminate green things, shimmering against a darker background—for a short time my skin can tolerate these slideshows in miniature, these private illuminations.

"What on earth is that?" I ask.

"It's beech leaves," he says indignantly, "in the spring."

"But it's completely out of focus."

"It's supposed to be out of focus. That's Art, that is."

"If that gets anywhere in tonight's competition," I say, "I shall be extremely surprised."

"Right," he replies. "Do you want to have a bet on that?"

I love bets. He knows I won't be able to resist. In the life before, I bet on all sorts of things—on the outcome of general elections, on who would win Wimbledon, on whether there would be snow before Christmas. Usually my bets were with friends and family—only once with Ladbrokes, when I was unable to get satisfaction elsewhere. A bet is a tribute to the unknowability of the future, an act of faith that the course of events may be probable, but is never fully determined. More than ever, now, I need them, I need that itch of hope.

"OK," I say, "let's have a bet. If that gets anywhere in tonight's competition, I'll . . . I don't know, what should the stake be?"

"After what you've said about my fine image, I think you should abase yourself."

"Hmm, that's a new one. OK, if you win, I undertake to abase myself. What about if I win?"

"I'll get us fish and chips at the weekend."

"Right. It's a deal."

Pete goes off to camera club. I pass the evening in the company of Agatha Christie, restlessly shifting position, trying to resist doing what would be most comfortable and natural, which would be to lie down on the bed. Finally I push the button on my little alarm clock and a small light illuminates its face. I see with relief that it is ten o'clock. I get washed, undressed and climb under the quilt.

At half past ten Pete knocks on the door and wakes me from my doze. "Hello," I say sleepily. I have forgotten all about our bet.

"Well, darling," he says, kneeling down beside my pillow, "I'm afraid you're going to have to abase yourself. My picture was highly commended."

"WHAT?" I roar, shooting upwards out of the bed. "But that's outrageous. Are you sure?"

"Of course I'm sure."

"What on earth was the judge thinking?"

"The judge was a highly discerning individual with excellent taste."

"Well, really," I snort. "That's completely bonkers."

"Perhaps he was glad to see something that was not a long-bodied chaser. Anyway, I still win."

"OK, OK, I'll do something about it tomorrow."

Actually, as it turns out, I do something about it sooner than that. Despite my efforts to mark out a boundary between day and night, to persuade my body of a qualitative difference between similar periods of blackness, I wake, as so often, in the empty early morning, and cannot find sleep again.

I decide to compose a "Song of Self-Abasement,"

and it absorbs and infuriates me, for hours. I push and shove words into lines, but they refuse to fit, bulging uncontrollably in the middle or drooping unaesthetically off the ends.

I am on the point of giving up when there is an audible "click" inside my head and suddenly everything has fallen into place. My words are standing neatly to attention, and none of them is mucking about. I open my eyes wide with surprise, and recite the whole thing through twice, to make sure I am not imagining it:

> My darling and Lord of my heart
> I accept that you know about Art
> Or at least that you know
> What a Judge in a Show
> Might consider as looking the part.
>
> My darling I'm down on the ground
> Confessing your judgement is sound
> And your eye for a pic
> Is both subtle and quick
> And your nose as acute as a hound.

I smile to myself in the darkness, and sleep slips over me at last, like a smooth incoming tide.

Metaphor

Some people believe that illness is a corporeal metaphor for the condition of the psyche. In their eyes, a problem in the back indicates an inability to put the past behind one; a failure to process old emotion manifests in constricted bowels.

It is my misfortune to have a condition which is peculiarly susceptible to metaphor. I prove irresistible to those of a vaguely New Agey turn of mind; they become tremendously excited when they hear about me. Here is something they have not come across before, surely a metaphorical manifestation par excellence. To cut oneself off from society, to insist on living in the dark in a sealed-up room—it is almost too perfect. Clearly I am terrified of human contact, indeed, afraid of life itself, desiring subconsciously to reverse the event of my own birth, and retreat to the dark close quarters of the womb.

What a fascinatingly damaged psyche! What I must do is *work on myself* (somehow, in the dark, on my own) and *address my outstanding emotional issues* (if I could work out what these were, apart from a frustrated desire to get out of the dark).

A reiki healer comes to see me, recommended by a friend. I lie on my bed and the healer moves her hands over me. It is pleasant and relaxing, until the metaphors kick in.

"I wonder," says the healer, "when you're in the light, do you feel . . . exposed?"

"Exposed?"

"Open to people's gaze, lots of eyes looking at you."

"What I feel is, I'd better get out of this light before I have a painful skin reaction," I say, "which, given my experience, is a pretty rational response."

More work is done on my chakras. I drift into a dreamy meditative state.

"And your partner," says the healer. "I suppose he has to do a lot of caring for you."

"Yes, he does."

"And how is he about that?"

"He's great. I think he's amazing."

"I'm wondering whether, perhaps, somewhere in your mind, you've got the idea that 'this relationship only works if I'm ill'?"

"I don't think so," I reply wearily. "We generally had a much nicer time when I wasn't."

The healing session continues, and I relax once more.

"Well, there's always a benefit, isn't there," says the healer, "even when it's really hard to see it."

"A benefit?"

"A benefit to having an illness. The deep reason why we keep having it."

I want to leap from the bed, put my SAS training into practice, and smash the woman in the face.

In such persons I diagnose a pathology of hypersignificance, an obsessive need to find meaning and pattern in human lives. Those afflicted with this disorder are psychologically unable to accept the extent to which we are embodied in physical reality, liable to be knocked about by the inheritance of some genetic susceptibility, by unwitting exposure to environmental risk factors, by the bizarre concatenations of chance. The novels of our lives are written only partly by ourselves; other forces regularly grab the pen, interpolating strange deviations and digressions, enforced changes of pace, character or plot.

But even while they are doing this, we retain some control over the quality of the prose. In the end we have one choice: to suffer well or suffer badly, to reach for or to reject that quality which is termed, equally, by both religious and secular, grace.

Parallels

I would like to hear about other lives like mine. But I can find almost nothing written; even when people undertake Internet searches on my behalf they turn up only traces: an article in a nutritional journal; a chapter in a Swedish book; a brief mention of a woman with porphyria who listened all day to talking books—always descriptions from the outside, and never from within.

So I have assembled a collection of parallels distilled from my hours of incessant, incontinent listening, from that random parade of whodunnits and thrillers, histories, romances and memoirs that have spooled through the darkness beside me, and have become my window (however weirdly coloured, dirty or distorting) on the world.

I covet tales of human beings in extremis; want to know how they felt, what they did, how they bore it. I collect confinements, deprivations, degradations *that last;* I thirst for descriptions of the bearing of the unbearable, day after day, the flickering on of life in situations which, looked at from outside, invite merely horror, and the expectation of abandonment through suicide or despair.

My collection fascinates me. It is a set of polished pebbles, stored in a snug velvet pouch in my mind. From time to time I tip them out to examine them, turn them over and over, feel their relative weights and textures, experiment with order and with pattern. I am using them to think with, to map out the contours of my own predicament, to develop standards of comparison. Each has elements in common with my own situation, although it is not the same.

There are four parallels in all:

1. *Notre Dame de Paris* by Victor Hugo, a book rich in strange and terrible confinements. The King, Louis XI, keeps a man in a cage; he was once the Bishop of Verdun. He has been in the cage for years, in a room in the Bastille. He pleads with whoever passes to intercede for him. The king will never let him out.

On the Grève, in a stone tower of the Tour Rolande, a penitent, years ago, walled herself in. A single small barred window opens on to the street outside through which people occasionally pass water and food. Mostly she sits on the straw of her cell and weeps for the loss of her child. She has been there sixteen years.

Under the fortress of the Tournelle lie the dungeons; under the dungeons lies the deepest, darkest pit of all. The only entrance is through a trap door. There is no light or warmth; the walls and floor exude a cold and liquid discharge; once a prisoner is confined there, that is the end.

For this is the oubliette, where people are placed to be *oublié*—that is, to be forgotten.

2. *The Innocent Man* by John Grisham describes a miscarriage of justice in small-town America. It is a true story. The book includes an account of the facility for Death Row prisoners at the Oklahoma state prison in McAlester. When it was opened in 1993, it was held to be the most modern, hi-tech and secure of its kind.

The building was entirely underground; the prisoners never saw natural light. The cells, and the furniture in them, were made of concrete. The concrete was never plastered over or painted, so the prisoners permanently breathed concrete dust. The "closed" ventilation system, which allowed no air in from the outside, frequently broke down. No one cared about the prisoners' health—hey, they were going to die anyway, right? But many lived on the Row year after year, as appeals ground their way through the system.

3. *The Secret Hunters* by Ranulph Fiennes, a novelisation of documents apparently found in a hut in Antarctica, telling how ex-Nazis try to found a new Reich funded by a secret Antarctic gold seam, but are pursued by a man who had escaped the Holocaust when he was a boy.

The book contains a description of Auschwitz.

None of the facts are new to me. I have been told them, taught them from early in my life. I have read books, watched documentaries, seen *Schindler's List*.

Somehow, nothing prepared me for this. Maybe it is the dark, or the first-person narrative, or my own mental state; but I am completely overwhelmed. It is the systematic humiliation before killing, the deliberate, conscious dehumanisation that grips me. My heart races and my breath comes in flickering waves, filling and emptying only the top tenth of my lungs. My torso is wrapped in iron; and the plates squeeze ever tighter together as if someone is tightening a screw. I know I should stop the machine, detach myself, relax, but it is as if the tape is passing physically through me, entering my skull through my left ear, slicing across through my brain. I cannot escape. I listen without a break, for hours.

4. *The Diving Bell and the Butterfly*, by Jean-Dominique Bauby. In his early forties, a journalist, the editor of *Elle* in Paris, has a massive stroke. When he regains consciousness he finds he is completely paralysed. He has what is known as "locked-in syndrome." He cannot move any part of his body—everything must be done for him. But his mind is alert and clear.

He finds that he can move one of his eyelids slightly. By blinking at the appropriate letter

as another person reads off the alphabet, he
finds he can, with the help of an amanuensis,
compose requests, remarks and finally the text
of this book.

I am impressed by Jean-Dominique Bauby. I think
about him a lot. I wonder whether, to enjoy as he does
the pleasure of sunsets, the trips out of the hospital to
the beach, the drawings and cards from his friends and
his children that decorate his room, the companionship
of the TV; whether, to gain, as it were, the benefits of
light, I would trade the movement of my body.

The pleasures of a body without light are not glam-
orous but, nonetheless, not negligible. I can go to the
lavatory when I please. I can eat when I choose and,
within the limits of what has been procured for me, the
food of my choice. I can savour my food. I can flex my
limbs, within the confines of my dark box. I can talk
freely to visitors, missing only the nuances of gesture
and expression.

In common, Bauby and I share the hunger for visits,
the long hours to be got through alone.

Would Bauby choose to swap fates with me, or I
with Bauby? Perhaps it is as well that life does not give
us such choices. We would spend hopeless hours with
our pens poised above the questionnaire, unable to
decide in which box to make our mark.

The worst part of the book, for me, is the afterword,
because that is when I find out that Jean-Dominique
Bauby is dead; that he died, in fact, in 1997, two years
and a few months after his stroke.

I am immeasurably distressed. I feel his death strongly, on behalf of all who lead impossible lives. It is too neat an ending, too easy a let-out for those who read his story, providing convenient closure, when, actually, for many there is none—just year after year of continuance, with the years blurring into each other, looping back on themselves, becoming hopelessly entangled in the mind, because the memorable events are so few and widely spaced upon the grey ropes of time.

Dream 4

I am in the bedroom of the flat in London where I used to live. It is a lovely room, facing south, with two large windows through which I can look down into the quiet street or up into suburban sky. In my dream, as in my memories, it is snug and warm, with sunbeams patterning the bristly brown carpet and dust particles dancing in iridescent swarms.

I sit on my bed with its crisp white sheets, and suddenly it is evening, the curtains are closed, and the room has become cold. Pete is there, with his head turned away so that I see only his profile. Someone else is also in the room, a woman in a short skirt and knee-high boots, with long straight brown hair cut across in a fringe. (I think the boots are unwise, because the woman has incredibly thin legs.) She is wandering about looking at my things, opening drawers, making comments on pictures, taking books off the shelves.

Pete, still not looking at me, is telling me that he is leaving me, that he regrets having to do it, but he knows I will understand.

I feel as though my heart, my lungs, my liver and my bowels have been gouged from the front of my body. Agony and emptiness invade me. I say nothing, cannot, in fact, say anything, just gaze at Pete's craggy profile and at his beautiful mouth as he speaks sensible, reasonable words, with which I can find no fault and make no argument. I am in shock, but I am not surprised. "So it's happened," I think to myself. "What shall I do now?"

And I wake in the darkness, believing the dream, and lie in bed rigid and panting, but with my mind already beginning to work, to chew over the remnants of my world.

I do not know how long I lie there, mourning and making plans. At last, tiny things start to burrow into my consciousness, carrying the pricklings of doubt. I hear the central heating come on with its characteristic hammer and grunt. I hear the bathroom door open and close, and the click of a light switch.

"Was I really in London?" I wonder, still half inside my dream. "In the light, in my flat? Surely that's impossible—that flat was sold a long time ago. And if I wasn't there, did any of it happen at all?"

And I remember how, years ago, a couple of months before I sat my A levels, I had a similar practice dream. In total, compelling detail, I dreamt that I received my results, and got three Ds, which made my planned course and university place impossible. I awoke, desperately disappointed and ashamed, and lay in bed for at least an hour, trying to work out what to do. I weighed up the pros and cons of resits, and wondered if I should stop trying to be an academic, and go to music college instead. I pushed my mind back to the exams themselves, hoping for a clue as to what had gone wrong—and found I had absolutely no memory of taking them.

Then I looked out of my window at soft spring drizzle falling on small-leaved trees, and my heart leapt as I realised that the future was still a clean page, its words yet to be written. But I was always grateful for the dream. It had given me a chance to practise my emotions, to experience in advance what, if the worst happened, they would be.

Strange Thoughts

In the pool of my mind, I find strange thoughts swimming. They flick across the corners of my inner eye, half-seen, yet distinct enough to allow identification.

Three separate species tenant these murky depths. There is the soft grey fish with scales of shadows, whose name, I find, is *envying the dead*. Each time I hear about a death, no matter whose—a relative, acquaintance, politician or some long-forgotten star—I feel within that sudden flash, that twist and plunge of jealousy. For the dead have already found their end, have found their turning from that long straight road; their story is complete, the last words written—the future can no longer terrify. They are enclosed both ends by time, wrapped in its gentle wadding, stored away as precious things. I still hurtle forwards on the cutting edge of chaos, into who knows what desolate and unexplored frontiers.

The second species is pale in colour; it drifts through the water like a reflection of the moon. Its name is *believing that you are a ghost;* it feeds on lengthy periods alone.

For hours, I cannot see the hand in front of my face; I cannot see my arms, my knees, my feet. In my box, I have no impact on the world, which travels on its course quite as if I were not in it. People pass the silent, shuttered house and, if they think at all, they probably conclude that it is empty. And what does dwell within? A thing that lurks, that creeps, that mopes, that wanders now and then from room to room, that flees in terror from the wide-flung welcoming front door, the joyful flicking-on of lights.

It is not surprising that I have delusions of nonexistence.

And, lastly, there's the thought that lurks at the bottom of the pool, where debris and slime have settled in layers, and the water is viscous and dim. It is an enormous pike, black and massive and strong, with spines along its back and rows of razor teeth. It can stay hidden for days, motionless in some mud hole, and I will catch no glimpses of its mottled, warty skin. But it will always re-emerge to float about the lower reaches of my soul. Its name, of course, is *suicide.*

The Means to an End

Most of the time, I do not want to die. But I would like to have the means of death within my grasp. I want to feel the luxury of choice, to know the answer to "How do I bear this?" need not always be "Endure."

I fret about the ways and means. I shrink from pain and violence, from mess, from the possibility of a botched job. I worry for the person who will find me, believe a still form on a bed would be less horrible than a bathtub full of blood. I am nervous of that period after the irrevocable act has been committed but before unconsciousness supervenes; in that intervening time, it is surely not impossible that your mind could change. How many suicides die in mental anguish, having clarified their true desires only by taking a drastic and irreversible step? There are no feedback forms beyond the grave.

I would like to have a stock of pills. I would keep them in the corner of a cupboard; they would be my insurance policy, their very presence easing my mind. But how do I obtain them? To phone my doctor and claim trouble sleeping is possible, but it is doubtful that the subterfuge could be sustained; my doctor knows my situation, and would swiftly smell a rat.

Then there is the wild world of the Internet, where, according to concerned voices on Radio 4, a multiplicity of sites offer detailed how-to guidance, chat rooms facilitate bonding with others also contemplating the exit, and online pharmacies supply the necessary dope.

There is a computer very close to my lair. It lives, in fact, in the room next door. But for me it is a shuttered, silent portal—screens burn me faster and more horribly than virtually anything else. I need an intermediary to surf the superhighway, and intermediaries are not, unfortunately, automata, but have thoughts and feelings of their own. Even if I could find one sufficiently indifferent to help me, it is unlikely that they would be blasé about the legal consequences.

So my stock of pills remains a pipe dream. Instead, I must formulate an insurance policy using materials that are to hand. In the kitchen drawer lie knives and a sharpening tool. My plan would be to file the longest to exquisite sharpness, and then, like the ancient Romans, fall on my sword.

It is amazing how much better I feel, once I have worked this out.

I WOULD LIKE to talk about suicide, but it is very, very hard; even more than death itself, this is the ultimate taboo. It touches people's rawest, most secret parts, throwing up questions about the value of a life; about what can be stripped away before it is no longer worth the living; about what they might have done, or have not done, to make my days more bearable; about how they might act, how they might feel, if they were in my place.

So, mostly, I try not to mention it. But sometimes, I feel that if I do not then I will burst with despair. Pressure builds within me, over a period of time, and there is only one release: to say, "I think I'm going to kill myself" and to say it to a listening ear.

People respond in very different ways. There is always a moment of shocked silence, which is how I know I have said the unsayable, broken some unwritten rule, taken my pants off in a public place.

My friend Ellen says, when I come out with my statement abruptly one day when we are talking on the phone, "Oh, but Pete would be so upset, wouldn't he, if you did that."

"He may be upset in the short term," I reply, "but in the long term he would benefit. It would set him free."

"Oh, I'm sure he wouldn't think like that."

But I am not so sure. And I soon change the subject, because I feel I am not getting an adequate response. I need something harder and firmer than the temporary feelings of a lover on which to build a case for my continuance.

When I make my statement to my brother, his reaction is simple and direct. "Don't do that," he says. "It would break our hearts."

His answer moves me to tears. But when I say it to my mother, she replies, "Well, I'd rather you didn't, but ultimately it's your choice."

I am shocked. I feel as if she has just hit me. Surely this is not what mothers are supposed to say—they are supposed to weep, and plead, and tell you how much they would miss you.

But there is history here, a complex and tragic tale. When I was small, my mother's own mother developed motor neurone disease. It is the disease which laughs in the face of the hospice movement and the advocates of palliative care: the victim gradually loses the movement of all their muscles, and ends up in a prolonged state of stalemate—not dying, but unable to swallow, excrete or communicate. There is little that can be done now to relieve this horror; in the early seventies, there was less.

My grandmother, who was fifty-eight, begged my mother to kill her, over and over again, until she could no longer form the words. My mother told me she was tempted to do it, but then she thought about me; she did not want me to grow up with a mother in prison. Eventually my grandmother was admitted to hospital, and the staff put her bed near an open window. As they had hoped, she caught pneumonia and finally, in that slow suffocation, passed away.

The experience made my mother a powerful advocate of voluntary euthanasia. She became a member of the Voluntary Euthanasia Society, which later became Dignity in Dying. Occasionally she would speak about what happened to the media; she also completed an advance directive relating to herself specifying the circumstances in which she would not wish further medical treatment. At the core of her argument was the sacredness of personal choice: facing the same set of terminal circumstances, each individual will choose differently; some may want to continue to their last breath, others may want to take an earlier exit. What is more, what a person believes they will want in such a situation may well change when they are actually in it; the individual who has spoken for years about a swift resort, should they reach a particular state of decrepitude, to a bottle of whisky and a packet of pills, may well end up dying slowly and naturally, having found that they value every last second of consciousness, even if only to observe the flickering lights on a hospital ceiling. Conversely, a person formerly convinced they could never desire to end their life could, as their guts rot and their sphincters fail, find their perspective altered. The point is that it is never for a person outside the situation to judge.

So I should not be shocked to hear my mother articulate a principle so deeply held. Or perhaps she is simply calling my bluff, suspecting that my intention is not really settled or serious, and that this is the best way to get me to snap out of it.

But the person, of course, who has to listen to my statement most often is Pete, although I do my best to keep it in. He takes a dim view of suicide. "It is against the rules," he says gruffly, "and ought to be against the law. It is extremely unfair on the people who are left behind." And if I continue to bleat on, "Don't do that, darling, I'd miss you."

Then, one day, I am put into the receiver's position. I have to respond to the statement myself. I am on the phone to one of my telephone friends, chronically ill, homeless and having a particularly bad time, and he says, "I don't know if I can carry on. I'm thinking seriously about suicide."

I do not hesitate. "I know what you mean," I say, "I think about it too. But really, you shouldn't. It would be letting the side down." I listen with surprise to the bracing quality of my own advice—but I find that this is really what I feel: that there is a duty of solidarity among all us impossible, near-invisible people; a duty, out of sheer cussedness, not to disappear completely, simply to ease the conscience of the rest.

And then I find myself telling my friend how years ago, in the life before, I went to Bristol to visit a girl I knew from university who was studying there to become a doctor. She took me to see the famous Clifton Suspension Bridge, a vertiginous feat of Victorian engineering spanning the deep gorge of the River Avon. As we walked on to it she pointed over the side, remarking ghoulishly, "That's where people jump off."

My stomach rolled as I looked down at a bare patch in the lush grass of the riverbank; it must have been a drop of several hundred feet. She went on: "Did you know, the suicide rate in parts of Bristol on a direct bus route to the bridge is much higher than the rate in places where you have to change?"

"Goodness," I said, finding this very amusing, full of the blithe contempt of youth. "People can't want to kill themselves that much, if they get put off because they have to change buses."

But that is, of course, the point. It is an impulse that may well not be sustained, if the person is given the opportunity to reflect. Other statistics bear this out: the fall in paracetamol overdoses, for example, when the pills were no longer available loose, in large bottles, instead having to be prised individually from smaller blister packs.

It cannot be common for statistics to save lives, but both I and my friend seem comforted by these.

Games to Play in the Dark 5: Scribe

This is a game to play on your own, when talking books have palled, when you have no visitors in prospect, when boredom eats your brain.

You will need a large bound notebook and a pencil. A bound notebook so that your pages are disciplined and do not become entangled. A pencil, because a pen could run out and in the dark you will not be able to tell.

Pick up your pencil and open your notebook.

Place the thumb of your non-writing hand on the page beneath the start of the first line.

Your thumb will act as a marker, so that there will be space between each line and the next.

Write.

Write what?

Write what you know. Isn't that what they say?

What you know is the darkness.

And as you begin to form words on the page, the darkness around you *moves*. It starts to gather, to circle, to form a vortex round the end of your pencil, and then—down the pencil's black centre it pours.

It is unstoppable. It flows faster and faster, funnelling down that slim conductive wand, erupting on to the page, staining its purity with straggling struggling words.

And in your mind, a light goes on.

The Unthinkable Future

There is no longer a road between me and my dreams. My dreams do not disappear—they float somewhere high up and off to the side, in a warm bright bubble untethered from the earth. To reach them from the here and now is inconceivable; there is no connecting path.

If I dare to look into the future, my own mind censors me, dropping a heavy black curtain across the pathway of the first tentative thought. My mind is kind—it has become wise in the ways of self-protection. It knows that to permit contemplation of the future is the fastest way to dissolution and despair. For what can lurk beyond that curtain? Only three things: improvement, deterioration or continuance, and two of these three, if they were to be known for certain, could not be borne. They are sustainable, in fact, only through ignorance.

It is a blessing to live on the cutting edge of time, with all that is before us hidden. Stop your ears to psychics, gypsies and angels; banish any who might claim to lift that veil. Orpheus rescuing his love from Hades glanced behind him as he climbed the upward slope, and all was lost. I get through my days by walking backwards; for me, the fatal thing would be to risk a forward look.

Part Two

Remission

The first signs are infinitesimal, almost imperceptible.

I come out of my room on one of my usual brief forays. I walk carefully down the stairs, thread my way through the gloom of the living room, surface in the kitchen, move swiftly to wash myself an apple and make a cup of green tea. I go back into the living room, sit down as usual at the dining table, bite into the cool sharp flesh of the apple, let the steam from the tea warm my nose. My eyes wander over the shapes in the murky room—some pale-coloured flowers in a vase, the spines of books on a bookshelf making a giant barcode of vertical lines. I chew on my apple, sip at my tea, and my thoughts drift.

And slowly, slowly I become aware that something that should, by now, be happening—is not happening. The ominous muttering in my skin that I have become conditioned to expect, since those first perplexing days at my computer so many months ago—it is not there.

I can scarcely believe it. I can scarcely allow myself to believe it. I slowly get up from the table. I have to put a hand to the wall to steady myself as my mind whirls. What should I do? How should I best use this extraordinary and incredible period of grace? In the end I decide that I should take exercise. I move some furniture out of the way, and in my quiet skin and rustling skirts, I pace up and down the living room, as if it were the long gallery of an Elizabethan country house, and I a lady stretching my legs on an inclement afternoon.

Then, after a while, the familiar prickling and tingling starts up, and I withdraw.

Back in my darkness I try to forget what has happened. It feels absurdly dangerous to let it linger in the mind—a spark set too close to huge silent receptacles containing that most flammable of substances, quiescent hope.

But the next day, the same thing happens again. I can go from total blackness into the gloom downstairs—and stay there for a while. There is an interval of silence during which my skin remains quiet, before the ominous murmuring starts up again, and I must once more be prudent, and withdraw.

And that is the first thing.

Days pass.

The second thing is that, while I am downstairs in the gloom, I can pull back one end of one long velvet curtain, and let in a feeble spindly shaft of day.

If I sit in a particular place, not too near the window and not too far away, and hold a magazine up close to my face, twisting my body round at an angle so that light falls directly on the page at which I peer, the words are legible to me. I get a pain in my spine and a crick in my neck, but the tickle of text against my optic nerve is a sensuous pleasure, a long-forgotten caress.

I sit and read the magazine.

Days pass.

I stay downstairs a little longer. I pull back the curtain a little further.

Then comes the third thing. It is momentous.

One evening, after dark, I put on my boots, hat and coat, and open the back door of the house. I step out on to stone flags in a small enclosed space. The wall of next door's kitchen is to my right, the wall of my own to my left, behind me the back wall of the garage, with a white-painted door.

But above me, a rectangle of clouded autumn sky, and before me, a path between bushes, drawing me on.

The smell of the world enfolds me. I grab great snorting gasps of the succulent night air, as though I am suddenly surfacing after being presumed drowned. I walk out on to the lawn, my legs shaking slightly, unused to such extended forward motion after so long a period of interior creeping. I move round and round the perimeter of the garden, relishing the unaccustomed swing of my legs, the roll of my feet, the movement of air against the skin of my face.

I could happily circle the lawn all night. But a street light lurks beyond the back fence—I must carefully measure my pleasure. After a few turns, I go back into the house. All the next day, I long for the evening, when I can try it again.

Rain

A few days later, I go out into the garden for my night-time walk, and find that rain is falling.

From the crown of my hat to the toes of my boots, an indescribable thrill runs through me. I stand poised at the edge of the lawn, and my starved senses open to this delicious, half-forgotten joy. Behind me the rain roars like a waterfall from the leaky gutter to the flat conservatory roof; it gurgles down the downpipes to the drains. I let it cover me. I let myself be soaked. Like a young plant, I let myself be watered well in. It is as though I am being kissed by the world, welcomed back to life.

On the other side of the little valley that runs behind our back fence is a chorus line of tall trees; I watch them as they wave their arms gracefully in time with the wind. In the garden itself, erratic branches from the dark-leaved cherry, a twisted wild-haired specimen, like a giant unkempt head, thrust frantically at odd angles. The feathery spire of the corner cypress splits and reforms, dusting the clouded, street-lamp-tinged sky.

My cap is weighing on my head, the hair underneath it hanging in rats' tails. Rain has found an opening at the back of my neck and insinuates itself inside, inching down my vertebrae in a cool, stealthy stream. Drops mottle the lenses of my spectacles and set the skin on my face tingling; I tilt my head upwards to catch more. Unintentionally I breathe rain into my nostrils and gasp; yet the water, though surprising, feels mild and sweet inside my tubes, different from memories of inhaling swimming pools and the sea.

I start to circle the lawn. A skin of surface water slaps beneath my soles. The lower part of my long silk skirt grows wetter and wetter, winding itself round my shins, catching under my feet, pulling ever more heavily on its elastic waistband as it slides inexorably over my hips. I hoick the garment back upwards, but the folds of silk are so swamped that each time it soon recommences its descent. I am put in mind of the heroines of nineteenth-century novels, and reflect on how inconvenient it must have been to stride about the countryside swathed in long skirts.

Eventually the irritation starts to detract from the intensity of the experience, and I go back indoors. "I've been relating to the rain," I say to Pete, breathless and exhilarated, as I stand in the kitchen with water pouring off me, like a dog that has emerged from a pond.

"Yes, I can see that, darling," he replies, as puddles form on the linoleum. "Personally, I've been staying indoors."

He has always had an unromantic attitude to rain.

Early in our acquaintance we went on holiday to Exmoor, and it rained most of the time, an intense threadlike downpour which soaked us as efficiently as a power shower. When it was not raining, the sky was a lugubrious unrelieved grey. I insisted on going for walks across soggy moorland, on the principle that we were in the countryside and ought to make the most of it. Pete was dour and monosyllabic inside his anorak. When we took refuge in pubs and tearooms, he complained ceaselessly about the weather. I began to find this mind-blowingly, relationship-threateningly boring, and eventually we had words.

He explained that his weather obsession was largely to do with opportunities for photography, and that he would also have complained, albeit not so much, if the sky had been unremittingly blue. What landscape photographers crave is good light—interesting light, the kind that comes from a mixture of cloud and sun; a break in the clouds towards evening, say, that throws a warm apricot glow on to boulders on a hillside; or a serendipitous shaft falling on a lonely tree beneath a stormy sky.

I looked at him across the table in the pub, and said, with a sudden access of clarity: "I think you'd sell your soul to the Devil for good light."

And Pete, respectable citizen, supporter of charities and follower of rules, said, "Hmmm. D'you know, I'd definitely have to think about it."

Astronomy

One evening, I go out to the garden for my walk, tip my face up towards a crisp, fresh-washed sky, and see stars.

Over London, the skies were fuddled with light. Windows, street lamps and headlights, advertising hoardings and road signs—all leaked radiance upwards and outwards, like smoke. Rare dark spaces were zones to traverse quickly, senses alert for following footsteps;

there was no time to notice what went on above my head.

Now, each night, I go out to meet the stars, and am disappointed when, because of cloud, they do not keep our date. I track their creeping trails across the sky as they make their nightly journey from east to west, starting each time from a slightly different place. It is like standing inside a giant hollow sphere, held and slowly turned by an enormous subtle hand.

I know one constellation. I recognise the three stars that make up the belt of Orion, in their neat diagonal line, and the four stars in a rough quadrilateral that form his limbs. Pete is much more knowledgeable, having been an enthusiastic stargazer when he was a boy. He still has his old telescope in the cupboard under the stairs—an unwieldy brute, consisting of a long white tube on extendable wooden legs, perpetually entangling itself with the ironing board, or the vacuum cleaner's hose.

One night he comes into the garden with me, allows me proudly to identify Orion, and then points out the different colours of its stars.

"See the one at the top left—it's more orange than the others. That's Betelgeuse. It's a red giant, relatively old and cold. And the one at the bottom right, in comparison, is—"

"Much more blue."

"Which is because it's a young star, much smaller and hotter. It's called Rigel."

"Wow—they're really different colours, when you come to look at them. Do you know, I think I'm getting astronomer's neck. There ought to be special angled leaning posts for contemplating the night sky."

Pete lets me lean back against him and holds me round the shoulders so my face is to the stars.

"What's the fuzzy bit below his belt?"

"That's the Orion nebula—a nursery of stars."

"Nursery?"

"An area where new stars are being formed. Basically, massive clouds of gas and dust. And if you follow his belt from right to left, and keep going in a straight line . . ."

"Yes, done that . . ."

"You'll get to Sirius—quite low down towards the horizon, which is the brightest star in the northern sky."

"Got it! Goodness, it's very twinkly."

"It is a particularly twinkly one."

Over the next few weeks, when the skies are clear Pete shows me how to find other stars. We buy an almanac that has a plan of the skies for each month and a list of notable astronomical events. I learn to locate Castor and Pollux, the two brightest stars in the constellation of Gemini; Taurus the bull, with its baleful red eye; Cancer, hard to see at all except on the clearest nights, when the faintest triangle sketches the face of the crab; and Leo, splendidly lion-like, with strongly outlined paws, mane and tail.

I am transfixed. I have never believed in astrology, but it is sheer joy to see those too-familiar names leap from the back pages of magazines and come to life in my own small patch of sky. It gives me a powerful sense of connection, not so much with the stars themselves as with my human ancestors. I sense them standing behind me in a long unbroken line, snaking back through millennia, through the Enlightenment, the Middle Ages, the Arabic and the classical world, back through the civilisations of the Babylonians and the ancient Egyptians, back to the first evolving consciousness that tilted its face to the heavens, saw these same strange shifting adornments, and felt compelled to make some sense of them. We are immeasurably better equipped, yet we are trying still.

One night Pete gets his telescope out from under the stairs. He sets it up on the lawn on its long unwieldy legs, which are secured in position by wing nuts and screws. I crouch down at a horrible back-wrenching angle, my knees sinking gently into cold damp earth, peer up the tube he has positioned, and see—

I see the planet Jupiter, glowing like a glorious cosmic orange, *and it is not alone.*

Three smaller discs are gathered round—three out of its four largest moons, the remaining one out of sight on the gas giant's far side.

These are the Galilean satellites—huge, diverse and strange, Callisto and Ganymede bigger than Mercury, Europa and Io only slightly smaller; what Galileo saw, when he turned his telescope on Jupiter, in 1610. Intrigued, he made a series of observations, which showed beyond doubt that the discs were moons, and that they were in orbit around the planet. This was how he refuted one of the key tenets of the Aristotelian universe: that all heavenly bodies must circle the earth.

A tremor passes through me, from my cricked neck

to my wet knees. For a moment, I feel as if I am Galileo, seeing for the first time with human eyes these specks that are mysterious new worlds.

It is a strange and fleeting conjunction, flavoured with melancholy and awe, an apprehension of the continuity of human wonder, and the brevity of human lives.

Remission Continued 1

Now that I have gained the freedom of the dark garden, the next thing—the fourth—is interior and domestic. By the light of a small lamp in the corner of the kitchen, made dimmer still by being placed behind the microwave, I prepare rice, fish and vegetables, wielding my knife gently to avoid slicing a fingertip.

I am cooking the dinner.

"I'm delighted you feel up to it, darling," says Pete, with enthusiasm, when he comes in from work. "We can have something edible for a change."

Pete, despite having had to do a lot of cooking, has neither started to enjoy it, nor become any better at it. He sits on a chair in the kitchen and watches me as I put the pan of rice on to boil, and lay the fish on a plate in the steamer, sprinkling it with thin strips of ginger and spring onion. I am making Chinese Steamed Fish.

"Cooking is so stressful," he says. "Take rice, for example. It ought to be impossible for rice to boil dry and be undercooked at the same time, but it isn't."

"Don't be silly," I say. "It's completely in accord with

the laws of physics for rice to boil dry and be under-cooked at the same time. Anyway, all you have to do is look at it now and then, to see how it's doing, and it won't."

"That's exactly what I object to," says Pete. "All this ad hoc adjustment and using your judgement. Cooking isn't rigorous."

"But you like making cakes," I point out. I mix soy sauce and sesame oil together in a little pan, and heat it gently.

"Cakes are different," replies Pete. "You mix up all the ingredients in a set formula and bung them in the oven at gas mark x for y minutes. None of this sloppy top-of-the-stove nonsense. Take that Nigel Slater omelette recipe. It said, 'Cook until the underside of the omelette starts to brown.' How was I supposed to know what the underside was doing—it was underneath."

"Well, it still wasn't a bad omelette," I say, because I aim to be encouraging, as I take the sauce off the heat.

"Recipes don't contain enough instructions," says Pete. "They could do with a few more Do-while loops."

"What?" I ask.

Pete explains about Do-while loops. They are programming commands in the computer language FORTRAN.

"Look," I say, lifting the lid of the steamer and poking inside with a knife, "could you stop talking a minute, or set the table, or something. I'm trying to exercise my judgement on this fish."

THE FIFTH THING is risky. Not all the variables are within my control. An unexpected encounter could send me back to the darkness to burn for several days. But I yearn to attempt it.

So I put on my boots, hat and coat, and this time I open the front door rather than the back, and step into the night-time close.

A person watching me would be puzzled by my trajectory. First I walk flush to one side of the driveway, pressed up against the bushes, and, when I reach the pavement, turn sharp right. Then I meander up the close, weaving across the road from side to side several times. When a car approaches, I leap behind a convenient shrub, or, if there is not one to hand, take to my heels.

The explanation is not, in fact, obscure. My next-door neighbours have a security light over their garage door, white, intense and horrible, easily tripped by casually passing down the drive unless one shimmies close to the furthest side. In the street I snake between street lights, not wanting to pass directly underneath their beams. Car headlights are the worst, particularly the newer bluer kind. They pierce my body like a pair of steel spears, drilling into my organs, into my bones themselves. So as I walk the night-time close I am constantly on the alert for the thrum of an approaching engine. Sometimes a waiting, idling car or the tripping of a security light mean I am trapped, and have to lurk suspiciously in some shadowy place for ages before I can make my way back to the house.

I have never walked by night in the African bush.

But I wonder whether my nocturnal navigations of the close bear certain similarities in the variety of potential hazards, the constant vigilance for large predators, the need for careful and circumspect advance.

The sixth thing is fun. From the dark far end of our long through-lounge, Pete in an armchair between me and the TV, the screen reflected in a carefully positioned mirror, I watch *The Apprentice*.

I give myself up to it with total delight. I roar with laughter, shout out rude comments, become rampantly partisan, practically expire with tension during the final Boardroom scenes. Because of the mirror, I get to know all the participants backwards, their right and left sides reversed, so when I see a photograph in the newspaper, it is always unsettling.

The seventh thing is small, but significant. I exchange my bulky under-trousers for tight black leggings beneath my silken skirts. This is very nearly a convincing fashion statement. About the nether regions, I feel suddenly, shockingly normal.

Between each small advance, days pass. The majority of my time is still spent in darkness, keeping company with electric voices. But there are holes appearing in the covering, like the activity of moths upon a blanket. I can come downstairs for one hour, then two hours at a stretch. Slowly, unevenly, the holes are getting larger.

I often miscalculate my next move. I am playing a game with snakes but no ladders; frequently I slither back towards the first square on the board, and must restart the slow, laborious ascent. But at least there is change, there is movement. Stasis has been left behind.

One thing has been found that helps me, mentioned in a scientific paper that Pete tracks down online. It does not put an end to my ups and downs, but at all stages it takes the edge off my reactions.

The substance is beta carotene. It is a very powerful anti-oxidant, used to help various light-sensitivity conditions, because it partly mitigates the damage set off by light in the skin. To obtain any effect, according to a man who is a member of the British Porphyria Society, one has to take a lot. I have twenty pills a day. This is about one hundred times the recommended daily allowance, and I do hesitate before I begin, there being various vague hints online about liver damage. I try to get clear medical advice on whether it is appropriate to take in my case, and what precautions or monitoring would be wise, but no one is prepared to give a definitive opinion. In the end I decide I have little to lose.

There is one side-effect—shortly after taking it, the skin becomes slightly orange. I do not mind. Often, there's not enough light to see me properly anyway, and when there is—the orange look is favoured by WAGs and TV celebrities, even certain politicians, so why should I object? Mine, however, is only a pale mandarin-yogurt imitation of such deep-toned, fruity complexions.

Trip

Pete has to go away for work, for five days, unexpectedly, at the start of the following month.

"Oh Pete," I wail, when he tells me, "that's just a couple of weeks before you go on holiday to Skye."

He is booked on a photographic trip to the Scottish island organised by a specialist company; the group will be taken by minibus to all the good locations, where they will leap out and set up their equipment. "Doesn't that mean you all end up with the same picture?" I ask, puzzled, when he first describes this, but apparently it does not.

Having known about the trip for some time, I have painstakingly arranged for people to come and stay while he is not here. Now—now I face having to do it all over again, with shorter notice, and everyone's plans already in place.

"Do you have to go?" I ask Pete.

"Well, yes I do. I'm sorry about the lack of notice, I can't help it. This sometimes happens, with work."

"But—does it always have to be you? Don't they realise you have caring responsibilities? I don't know—supposing you had a sick child or something . . ."

He looks away. He has not, of course, said anything at work, or only in the most general terms. "Well, I could say that, I suppose, but I would rather not. Anyway, you are not as bad as you have been."

And this is true. Barring accidents, provided with food, and with a creative approach to when and how I do the washing up (the kitchen sink being by a window that faces south, and the blind only a partial barrier), I can function here, in the house, on my own. I do not need a carer. What I need is something more abstract and intangible: a human presence about the place, occasional company when I have to go into the black; company that understands my situation and cares enough to observe the protocols, waiting till I'm out of the room and closing the door prior to turning on overhead lights.

The next afternoon, I pick up the phone to my mother with a heavy coldness in my stomach.

"Mum, you know you were going to come and stay when Pete goes on holiday—"

"Oh yes, don't worry—it's in my diary, I've moved my pupils—it's all arranged. I'm coming for the first part of the week—I'm really looking forward to it—and then Sam's going to do Thursday night and Friday, and I think you've got Celeste coming at the weekend?"

"Yes . . . that'll be great . . . it's just . . . unfortunately—well, Pete's just told me he's got a five-day trip for work, two weeks before."

"What . . . you mean the sixth to the tenth?"

"Yes."

"The sixth to the tenth next month?"

"Yes."

"I wish you'd told me sooner. I've got pupils doing exams, and it's my recital on the fourteenth. I suppose Sam *might* be able to come, depending on his schedule. Isn't there anyone else?"

And there's the rub.

I hate this situation, this having to ask and plead. Faster than anything else, it makes me feel a total failure. Somehow, in my life before, I should have been more charismatic and popular, so that people, now, would cross counties to babysit me. I should have judged better, spread myself more thinly, not spent my time on intimate friendships that would not stand the test.

"How did you get on with your mum?" Pete asks, when he gets home from work.

I shrug hopelessly and my eyes fill with tears. "I think I'd prefer to cope on my own," I say. "I'm sure I'll manage. I just wish your holiday wasn't so soon afterwards."

"You know I have to have my holiday," says Pete. "If I didn't, I'd probably beat you up."

He would not, of course, but I know what he is trying to say.

Pete does not emote much. He very rarely shows anger or frustration at me or our situation, being more likely to get cross if the table is sticky, or I have left a mess of paper, books and mail-order packaging all over the living room. But it has to come out somewhere; he needs to go off and do stuff, and I have to let him.

His trips are a mini-holiday for me as well—having different people to stay means I consult different tastes regarding meals; use garlic and spices, on which Pete is not keen; eat later in the evening; sometimes even *leave the washing up entirely*, which Pete is constitutionally unable to do; watch other people's TV programmes; play piano duets and cards.

In the end, Sam comes for a couple of days, instead of coming when originally planned. I book an Alexander technique lesson for one morning, with my lovely teacher who comes to the house. Two telephone friends agree to phone. In case of emergencies, I have the number of the neighbour who is good at DIY (once, one of my visitors, conscientiously drawing the curtain, ripped the entire curtain rail away from the wall).

Pete phones me every day, sometimes more than once. "Can you hear that?" he says one evening. "I'm just beside the sea." From the handset comes a regular whoosh and rasp, like a giant's heavy breathing.

I am transported.

Remission Continued 2

The next step—the eighth—crosses a boundary: I venture out at twilight, and catch my first glimpse of a non-dark world, painted in subtle shades of grey.

Equipment is required in order to progress to the ninth thing. The human eye, because it is so instantly responsive to conditions, is very bad at judging absolute levels of light. I would like to venture forth a little earlier, to catch some colour in the world, before it drains away. But how to judge, in different seasons and under different skies, the amount of light to which I'll be exposed?

Once more I have reason to be grateful for Pete's photographic bent. "What you need is a light meter," he says, and procures me one from a technical website. It is a rectangular black palm-sized gadget, with a white half-sphere at one end to measure ambient light and a digital display on which the reading appears.

Pete sets it up in idiot mode, so that, unless I really put my mind to it, I cannot mess things up—and a whole new world of objective measurement opens its doors. "This evening I did f2.8 at one second," I say happily, having been in the garden a little after sunset, but before the world is monochrome. It is early June— I have looked at orange poppies and pink roses, and watered tomato plants like green and writhing snakes. The colours slam into my retinas like crossbow bolts— but it is sweet pain.

I learn the peculiar scale that light meters employ: f1 (almost dark) is followed by f1.4, f2, f2.8 then f4 (about when street lights come on), f5.6, f8 (the sun just above the horizon, if the sky is clear). Pete explains that each step up represents a doubling of the amount of light, so I should be prudent when attempting to move from one level to the next. He also, lest I get too excited, points out that light levels at noon are f200 plus; I am taking baby steps, nibbling at the edges of the day.

Nevertheless, I am thrilled to have a way to track my progress. I note down in my diary each evening the f-number at which I went out. When people ask me how I am, I reply at first with incomprehensible technical blather, describing how I "managed f8 yesterday and hope to try f16 at the weekend." Only photographers understand.

My diary has a useful page showing sunrise and sunset times for each week of the year. This is very helpful for me, as I can work out at around what time I should start preparing for my walk. I have become a dusk-tracker, an adherent of planetary rather than human time, following the swing of the earth as it loops around its star. My slice of dusk moves through the day, its contents changing with the seasons as the days contract and dilate like the slow pupil of an eye. In winter I coincide with children in scarves and hats walking home from school; at equinoxes, with the return of car-borne commuters to suburban driveways; in April and August, with the hour of soap, when there are few people abroad and giant TV screens effloresce from the walls or corners of front rooms. Around midsummer I must wait and wait for hours, far into the evening, as a fiery teardrop slides down the blue cheek of the sky.

Encounter

One day I go out for my evening walk at f8, according to my light meter. I wander for a while among the houses, then cut down a path which leads to open ground. A stream in a concrete culvert runs through the estate, and the developers have left a broad area of grass along either side, with occasional trees and hawthorn bushes, so that the whole forms a sort of miniature valley where people stroll or walk their dogs, and children ride their bikes.

I turn on to the path beside the stream—and stop in my tracks.

There, just above the horizon, oozing dark crimson into flesh-coloured cloud—a giant inflamed eye.

For the first time since the darkness, I have come face to face with the sun.

I look at the sun. The sun looks at me. Something indescribable passes between us.

It is a first parley between old, old enemies. It is coming across a former lover suddenly, in the street, years after they broke your heart. It is sitting down to negotiate with terrorists, looking across the table into the eyes of a killer, knowing that the two of you are locked in this thing together, and some modus vivendi must be found.

I stand on the path by the stream. I extend my hand to the horizon.

"Hello, sun," I say.

Puppy Cage

What I would like to do is find a way to travel for a while *before* dusk to a scenic spot so that when my time comes I can burst forth and enjoy my walk somewhere new.

But how is this to be done? Dracula travelled from Transylvania to Whitby in one of a consignment of coffins; he came out each night to prowl about the ship and feast upon the crew.

A coffin, however, is not practicable. There could be difficulties breathing, and it would not fit in the car. Instead, Pete and I devise a contraption that can be installed and uninstalled in the back seat. It consists of a large piece of industrial felt, black, half a centimetre thick, and two long wires. According to the photobiology department at the hospital I once attended, high-quality black felt is the most light-protective material. The wires are strung between the grab handles which sit above each of the back doors. They pass in and out of holes in the felt, so that they hold it up. The forward part of the felt hangs over the back of the front passenger seat.

The result is a sort of small tent in which I can sit while being driven about the countryside. My friend Pam christens it the Puppy Cage.

Now my horizons expand. I consult my table of dusks and dawns, subtract the amount of time before sunset that I can currently manage, and estimate the length of the journey to the common or woods I have in mind. This tells me when we'll need to leave the house. Then I subtract a further ten minutes to allow for wrestling with the puppy cage. Unfortunately this is something Pete has to do on his own. The felt is heavy and unwieldy, and the green wires stick out of it like tentacles. A person watching him manoeuvre it towards and then into the car would conclude he was fighting to the death with a slightly home-made-looking monster, perhaps from an early series of *Doctor Who*.

Once the damn thing is in place, Pete gives a signal to me. In my hat, coat and boots I charge out of the house and nosedive into the open back door of the car, burrowing under the folds of the felt. I flail about for a while finding my seatbelt and disentangling my handbag straps, then, finally, we're off. I am sitting diagonally behind Pete, and encased in heavy material, so conversation is muffled. It is difficult to pass casual remarks without having to roar them at a volume out of proportion to their significance:

"Highland cows coming up on the right."

"What sort of nice house?"

"What?"

"What sort of house?"

"Not house, COWS."

"What?"

"Oh, never mind, we've gone past them."

"Gone past what?"

"HIGHLAND COWS."

"Oh, right."

Pause.

"I wonder what Highland cows are doing in Hampshire, anyway."

"Being hairy, I suppose."

"What?"

"BEING HAIRY."

And so on.

But it's all worth it when we get to the woods. I leap from my puppy cage, my nose glorying in a thousand different outdoor smells, and bound towards the freedom of the trees.

Word

crepuscular *a*. of twilight; (Zool.) appearing or active before sunrise or at dusk [f. L *crepusculum* twilight].

I discover that I have become crepuscular, and that I share this characteristic with various creatures, including deer, rabbits and short-eared owls.

Also wombats, apparently.

Honeypot

Growing up in London, I never went to the New Forest. It isn't very hilly, and my upbringing taught me to associate holidays and days out with strenuous ascents followed by contemplation of the world from a high vantage point, rather than the more tenebrous pleasures of trees.

Emerging from my darkness in Hampshire, however, I find the New Forest is a good place for expeditions. It is easy to get to, and the shade of the trees stretches the time I can be outside. I can start my dusk walk earlier than I could in open country, and stay out later after dawn.

I am impressed by the rugged girth of the ancient trees, their intense individuality, their fabulous lived-in look. Lattices of ivy stems cross-garter their lower trunks, mistletoe springs from out-flung limbs, holly bushes sprout between long gnarled toes. Lichens in understated greys and beige, and designer mosses, smooth as moleskin, or hairy like fake fur, patch their corrugated skins. Supersized fungi stud them, like jewels.

They stand at intervals, these huge bedecked trees. Smaller, younger trees grow between them, but it is clear that these are mere underlings assisting at the council of their elders, and do not really count. Pete and I wander past the ankles of the great, of no more moment than a cat that, during a conclave of cardinals, pads across the room.

Trees may well have matters to discuss. I have heard

of a mysterious occurrence that suggests co-operation between oak trees. Mice eat the acorns of oaks; a few fruitful years cause the mouse population to explode, and the chances of acorns eluding their attentions become small. But then there comes a year in which the oaks produce no acorns at all. Many mice die because they can find no food. In the years after the cull, acorns reappear. It works, of course, only if all oaks act together.

A CREPUSCULAR LIFE can lead to strange misapprehensions. Visiting the New Forest at dusk and dawn, Pete and I rarely see other people, coming across mainly ponies and deer. I comment on the absence of humans, which serves to render more striking the powerful presence of the trees.

"You do realise," says Pete, "that if we went in the daytime like normal people, the whole place would be jumping?"

"Really?" I say.

"Yes. It's a honeypot. Loads of people go there. Honestly, you are a nitwit. What did you think all those empty car parks were for?"

"Ah," I say. "I suppose there were a lot of car parks, actually, now one comes to think of it."

Mottisfont

I am always on the lookout for different things to do at dusk—new woods and paths within a reasonable distance of our home, outdoor concerts and theatre, if they do not start too early, and the audience is not overlit. Much research is needed, and often the idea does not come off.

"You should look into Mottisfont," says Pete. "They have a walled rose garden, and they open late for two weeks around midsummer, when the roses are at their peak, because so many people want to see them."

Eagerly I page through the National Trust handbook. Mottisfont is a property in the valley of the River Test, not too far away. Its rose garden is internationally famous, specialising in traditional old-fashioned varieties that have not had the smell bred out of them in pursuit of the structure or longevity of the blooms.

I run my finger down the table of opening times—and indeed, for two weeks, the gardens stay open until 8:30 p.m. But, consulting my diary for sunset times, I find that this is no good—because around the summer solstice the sun is at the peak of its glorious career and, diva-like, does not quit the stage until at least twenty past nine. Currently, I can manage half an hour before sunset—but that would mean starting any visit at 8:50 p.m., twenty minutes after the gardens have closed.

So near and yet so far, I think sadly, imagining roses that I will never see. I mind even more for Pete than for myself; I want to give him treats that we can enjoy together, as there is still so much he has to do alone.

So I decide that I have nothing to lose. I write a letter to Mottisfont explaining my situation and asking if there is any possibility that we could visit the garden later. I offer to pay for the inconvenience, or extra hours for staff.

It is early May when I write, and I fully expect to receive nothing but a polite refusal. But then, in mid-June, a lady phones me up. "I'm sorry we haven't got back to you," she says. "It is extremely busy here during the rose season. But yes—you can come. We can open the gardens for you between nine and ten, and there's no need to pay."

"That's wonderful," I say, overwhelmed. "Thank you so much."

So on the date agreed, I climb out of my puppy cage into a car park from which the last vehicles are dispersing after a long and sultry day. The air is warm and close, but the first cool tendrils of evening are beginning to lace their way through. Soon a young woman appears, with keys, and lets us into the main grounds. Together, we cross a stone bridge over the burbling river, then pass along the north front of the house, and past the stable block, and through an avenue of enormous stately trees, before we reach the walled garden itself.

The wall is high, and made of old bricks in an incredible variety of colours—russet, violet, peach and cream, the descending sun brushing all of them with gold. The young woman unlocks a door in the wall, and holds it back for us with her outstretched arm.

We go inside.

The smell wallops us in the face.

It is as though we have passed from air to some new substance, formed of a thousand interlocking scents that twist languorously about each other, like invisible smoke. We feel resistance on our skin as we push further in, as if the garden within the wall were at a higher pressure than the world outside. The temperature itself grows warmer. "There you are," says the young woman. "Enjoy! I'll meet you back at the front gate at around ten." She closes the door on us, and we are left alone in this magical, rainbow garden, trespassers in its silent, oozing profusion. To strike a match would probably be dangerous; the whole thing might explode.

We look slowly about us. A wide border runs all the way around the walls, backed by climbing plants spread-eagled across the brick. The main part of the garden is laid out in geometric beds, with long straight paths running between them. Some of these walks lead under arches, thick with climbing roses. At one crossroads is a circular stone pool, with a little fountain at its centre. Apart from the discreet bubbling of the water and the drone of late bees zigzagging between blooms, every-thing is still.

There are roses here—but many other flowers as well: lilies that thrust upwards on long slender spikes, tufted carpets of pinks, neat humps of lavender like green-and-purple porcupines; plants that fork and furl and splay, plants of which I do not know the names, plants with ordered, structured heads, plants with trail-ing, pendulous sprays.

I run my fingers gently along smooth and furry leaves, put my nose into velvet and silken depths. I want to get bodily into the beds, and roll; I have to hold myself back.

Slowly the light alters, from yellow to purple to blue. The colours in the garden grow softer and less distinct. Pete, who has been taking pictures, puts away his camera and comes to join me. We sit on a bench beside an enormous flesh-coloured rose, its blossoms blowsy and collapsing, revealing indecently hairy yellow centres. Petals spread over the earth and grass like a layer of delicate ears. The fragrance wraps us in a private cloud.

"We are very lucky to see this on our own," says Pete. "During the rose season there are usually hordes of visitors, and the whole place is packed."

There is evidence of hordes passing through: some of the paths are made of turf, which has been ground down into bare earth by hundreds of feet. And there is a sandwich on one of the seats, in a plastic triangular case.

"Yes—it's wonderful," I say, leaning back on the bench and looking at the sky, where a moon has appeared, like a suddenly opened eye. "Complete, decadent luxury." But I still feel a small pang. I would quite like to be part of a horde now and again, to rub up against my own species in the mass. It does not happen any more.

We wander back to the door in the wall, and slip through into the real world, closing it carefully behind us. We make our way through the shadowy grounds to the entrance, passing an elderly lady exercising a snuffling dog among the stately trees.

"She must live here, lucky person," I whisper to Pete.

"Yes," he replies, "I think there are apartments in the house."

The young woman with the keys is waiting at the gate. When we thank her, she tells us that it has not been any trouble, as she does not live far away. We drive back in the not-quite-dark midsummer night, and on the inside of my eyelids I carry with me the imprint of glorious flowers, and in my nostrils, the ghosts of their perfume.

Hats

I have always been a hat person, and now I have the perfect excuse for building a truly fine collection. The exercise bike in the corner of the living room, bought years ago by Pete in a keep-fit paroxysm but used only periodically by either of us since, has found its true vocation as a hatstand. Hats are piled up on the handlebars, hooked over the LCD display, and one sits proudly on the uncomfortable, buttock-slicing seat.

In my acquisition of hats I face one main obstacle, apart from the obvious difficulty of not being able to visit shops. I have a very large head, and thick hair; many hats do not fit, perching on top in a ridiculous manner, and resembling, as my mother puts it, "a pimple on a cheese."

I fall constantly for hats in catalogues that claim "one size fits all," and find, invariably, that it does not. Sadly, I package up the hat for Pete to take to the post office. He has to do this on Saturday mornings, when there is a long queue, and the whole process makes him grumpy.

"If you must purchase unsuitable hats," he says, as he pulls on his anorak, "can you at least try to do it from companies that offer a courier collection service?"

"But it was such a beautiful hat," I wail.

"Face it, darling, you haven't got a normal head." He stomps to the front door. "Now is this proof of posting or have I got to pay?"

Pete's goddaughter Sophie, who is six, comes to visit, accompanied by her parents, and by Hannah, her smaller, fiercer, faster-moving sister. We sit about chatting, drinking tea and eating cake. Slowly, as though drawn by an invisible magnetic field, the two little girls sidle towards the exercise bike. When they get close to it, Hannah, looking back to see if anyone is noticing, lifts off a hat and puts it on.

It is a large-brimmed hat in a brown woollen material, and it entirely envelops her head. She stands stock still, suddenly transformed into an oversized mushroom. Meanwhile, Sophie has selected a straw hat with a pink scarf round it, and is examining herself in the long mirror on the wall. Hannah, recovering from her surprise, throws off the brown hat and finds a black waterproof one decorated with a small flower, which she reaches up and places on her father.

Soon everybody is wearing hats.

Even the silly hat comes into play. It is a greyish-brown toque-like creation in stretchy fake fur, with a stripy Davy Crockett tail hanging down the back. Pete brought it back from a trip to the States—the hat is entirely useless in terms of light protection, but an excellent source of entertainment.

Sophie comes up to me and asks shyly, "What is your favourite hat?"

"That's a very good question," I say, and consider

the matter. Finally I pick out an oversized cap with a big peak, made of rich brown plush the colour of ginger cake. "This one. This is the one I like best."

Sophie nods approvingly. "That is a good hat," she says.

Despite their popularity with visiting children, my hats, worn on walks, have an unfortunate disadvantage. Dogs in general become excited by my presence; a subset of dogs, it turns out, have a particular susceptibility to hats.

Pete and I are getting out of the car one winter evening towards sunset, preparing to go for a walk in some snowy woods. We come across a man returning to his vehicle accompanied by a small, yappy dog. The dog takes one look at me, in my woollen, broad-brimmed hat, and launches itself at my throat.

Luckily, being a small dog, its powers of propulsion only take it to three or four times its actual height. I stand frozen with my back to a coppice of hazel as, barking fiercely, it bounces up and down to the level of my chest.

"Come here, Hugo," the owner, a scruffy, oddly dressed type, says lackadaisically. Then, when the dog takes no notice, he says accusingly, "It's your hat. He doesn't like your hat."

I smile weakly, expecting the man to call his dog off, but although he says, "Come here, Hugo," a couple more times, and opens the boot of his car, the dog continues to bounce, like a rubber ball with curving, miniature claws.

"He doesn't like hats," the man says again.

"Look," I say breathlessly, "I have to wear a hat for medical reasons. I would like to take it off, but I can't."

My heart is pounding and my legs are starting to shake; the dog seems to be gaining momentum, its snapping jaws getting closer to my face. Pete tries to distract it, and the man thumps the boot with his hand, calling it to get on board, but it is obsessed.

There is no one else in the tiny forest car park, a small tongue of mud and gravel off the side of a country road. Long yellow rays of low sun weave through the leafless trees; I feel them warm the back of my coat. I consider running, but I am standing on snow that has been compacted to lethal smoothness by many wheels and feet; the last thing I want to risk is a fall that would bring me within range of those teeth.

Despairingly I lift up my hand. I grasp the brim of my hat, and pull it down to my side, scrunching it in my fingers to try to conceal it from view. The sun encircles my head.

The dog subsides, barks cursorily a couple more times, jumps into the waiting boot. The man laughs, slams his door, and drives on his way. I replace the hat and we have our walk, but I do not escape the consequences: the next day, and several days afterwards, in the dark.

I ask everyone I know about dogs and hats. What is it that the dog thought it saw on top of my head? Or was it what it could not see—my eyes, perhaps, shadowed beneath the brim? The whole thing remains mysterious, serving only to increase my circumspection when I am out and about, and some low leaping form appears in my field of view.

Garden

I did not have much interest in growing things, in the life before. Emerging from the darkness into a light-limited, largely housebound life, I look about for occupation, and discover the garden. Plants do not mind being attended to at dusk; in fact, where watering is concerned, they actively like it. So long as I can go outside at f4 or above, it's safe to hack back branches and prune roses without risk to limbs. (I did try twilit weeding at f2, but, failing to distinguish leaf-shapes in the gloom, I unexpectedly grasped a nettle.)

The garden, when I first give it my attention, has been Pete's for several years. It is full of low-maintenance trees and shrubs, chosen because they have good colour in autumn, abundant blossom in spring, interesting seed heads, or some other feature of photographic interest. I can appreciate a good seed head as much as the next person, but I instinctively feel that something is missing. Apart from a lovely apple tree of the variety "Reverend W. Wilkes," which showers us most Augusts with huge, blushing cooking apples, there is nothing in the garden that we can EAT.

I start with herbs in pots. Then I move on to tomato plants in containers, potatoes in the old compost heap and Giant Russian sunflowers against the fence. Then I order a small raised bed, and plant salad leaves, radishes, rocket and strawberries. My army of containers slowly marches across the patio, until it is occupied completely, and surrenders.

I have more enthusiasm than expertise. One summer, I watch with interest as the fruit on one of my tomato plants ripens. Soon the plant is heavy with juicy yellow fruit. But I do not pick it, because I am expecting it to turn red, to match the picture on the plant label.

Not a spot of red appears. Finally I twig. I have a yellow tomato plant. I make the tomatoes into a golden salad. They are as sweet as plums.

I acquire a blueberry bush, but it does nothing at all. I am told by a friend that blueberries need to be grown in pairs, so that they can cross-pollinate. The next year, I acquire a second bush. In the spring, it starts to produce sprigs of white, globe-shaped flowers, with little frills round the bottom, like fancy lampshades. But the first blueberry is still refusing to play.

I phone the garden centre. "Do you have a blueberry bush which has flowers on now?" I ask. They do. I despatch Pete. "Secure that blueberry!" I tell him. We place all three pots together in a triangle—and a miracle occurs. Suddenly all the blueberries are blooming madly and, after having some form of group sex, produce a profusion of fruit.

I try to analyse why I have become so addicted to fruit and vegetable growing. It's partly a frustrated urge to be economically and socially useful: unable to undertake paid work to contribute to society, I can at least contribute food. It also gives me objects to care for outside myself which require my regular attention, whose health can be fretted over, and achievements praised, like pets or low-maintenance children. Sometimes I become so absorbed in the healthy growth of one of my charges that I almost forget to harvest it, having temporarily lost sight of the fact that, unlike pets or children, my plants are not what philosophers call "ends in themselves," but only means for the sustaining of other life.

Most of all, I like to feel the force of nature under my hands, to sense in a seed or a stem that coiled, compressed energy, that massive latent power, that thrust upwards and outwards which cracks concrete and crumbles masonry to dust, that raw lust for the sun. It reminds me that I too am part of nature, that the same power pulses in my veins, and I hope that whatever the obstacles it will keep pushing to straighten out the deformations of my skin, and point me, finally and irrevocably, towards the light.

Assistant

I want an assistant to help me use the computer. I decorate a small card with felt-tip pens. "Are you computer-literate?" it says, in curly pink and purple letters. I add a few flowers for good measure, a job description and my contact details. Pete puts the card up in Tesco. I receive many replies. I recruit a nice lady who comes once a week for two hours.

It is a varied job. Sometimes I need letters typing or emails sending. Sometimes I am interested in research papers on light sensitivity. Sometimes I have simply set my heart on a new hat.

Having an assistant means I no longer have to bother Pete to do online things for me. He looks at computers for most of his working day, and a large part of photography, in a digital age, involves fiddling with Photoshop.

I confine myself to limited communications and transactions. My emails are brisk and to the point. I can't afford to pay my assistant to engage on my behalf in the more spontaneous, interactive, weird and time-wasting aspects of the Web. It could also be rather embarrassing; what one might be quite willing to share electronically with thousands of anonymous strangers, one may still not wish to disclose to a nice lady sitting in the next room. Thus I forswear chat rooms, gambling, social networking and Internet porn. It is frustrating, but no doubt good for the soul.

My assistant, Claire, is quite posh. She has not worked since she got married in her mid-twenties and is now in her late forties, very attractive and well turned-out. Being short and petite, she always wears high heels— cowboy boots or tight leather boots in the winter and sandals when it's warm. She has four children, with fabulously posh names, and a dog called Harvey, whom she loves, and takes on walks for at least two hours each day.

She is always in the middle of some sort of interior design project in her home, worrying about builders, or the delivery of sofas, or the sourcing, for a fireplace, of marble of precisely the right shade. She has recently completed a computer course; I represent her first foray into modern office life.

Claire types my emails and letters with reasonable accuracy, plus a certain ditsy charm. Her favourite thing of all, however, is when I want to do Internet shopping, especially if it is for home accessories or clothes. She loves the challenge of tracking down the right sort of denim jacket (fully lined, hip-length, buttons most of the way up the front) or summer skirt (flared, no splits, non-flimsy material, length well below the knee).

The only problem is that her natural price point is set a little higher than mine, so she tends to gravitate first to sites selling cut-price designer labels, whereas I would probably start with Next and work up.

One morning Claire arrives wearing an unusual wraparound top. Some parts are blue and white stripes, some parts are blue spots on white, and others are white spots on blue.

"That's jolly," I say. "Is it from Boden?"

"Armani, actually," she replies, and we both collapse in fits of giggles.

Sometimes Claire brings me mail order catalogues for The White Company or Crew. Neither is quite my natural habitat, but our clash of consumer cultures is always stimulating. She scores a big hit with Laura Ashley, who turn out to sell exactly the right sort of lampshades for my small shielded low-level lamps, and she even offers to buy them for me when she is next in the nearest large town.

"Oh, it's no problem," she says. "I have to wait for Persephone to finish tennis practice, so there is plenty of time to look round the shops."

Of all the limitations of my life, I think it is my

inability to shop with which she empathises most—also, my dependence on Pete to procure random items which I cannot get mail order or online.

"There's simply no point sending a man to get these things," she says severely. "Even if you give them all kinds of instructions, they will never get it quite right, will they?"

She does her best to remedy the situation, with great kindness.

Music

I am back in my lair for one of the regular periods in the dark that break up my day. I am listening to a bizarrely unfunny comedy programme on Radio 4 and it's driving me wild. Suddenly, I can't stand it any more. I leap up and lay hands on my set. Somewhere out there, there has to be something better than this. I seize the knob and twiddle hard.

The "Ride of the Valkyries" storms out of the radio.

I fall about laughing—it is so unexpected—but I listen, and find I am enjoying it. Somehow I have regained my ability to listen to music alone, in my black room, without becoming an emotional basket case. The memory of departed joys, once so catastrophically evoked, threatens less now I can look forward to adding to my store. A weird inner wound, inflicted by the darkness, has healed, cauterised by the returning light.

Feet

One day my assistant Claire comes to do some computer work for me. I greet her with an enormous grin. "There's something different about me today," I say. "Can you spot it?"

My assistant looks me up and down. My hair's the same. My spectacles are the ones I've had for ages. I'm wearing clothes I've definitely worn before. Suddenly she sees it. "You've got feet!" my assistant cries.

There at the bottom of my long silk skirt, emerging from black-legging-clad legs, a pair of pale feet, flexing their toes against the carpet like newly hatched alien young.

I have managed to take off the nasty nylon socks I have been wearing for so long. (They are special light-protective socks, of a dense, stretchy, extra-fine fabric.) At first I only risk it for a couple of hours, then half a day. But gradually I build up. I'm not surprised that feet are the first thing I can uncover. Bony body parts— hands, face and skull—have been (thank goodness) less sensitive than fatter or more muscular ones, and I have not had to cover them. Feet are the obvious place to go next.

I am very proud of my new feet. I thrill to the sensation of carpet and linoleum against my bare soles. Even on chillier days, I am reluctant to put on socks, and give up the sight of my liberated toes.

Holiday

Having worn the house for so long, I would like to try on somewhere new. But I need my environment to be just so—with curtains and blinds to control what comes in the windows, the right sort of light bulbs for the evening, a blacked-out space to sleep in and for my periodic retreats during the day.

"What we need," says Pete, "is a caravan."

My family holidays were spent in rented cottages or youth hostels, which acted as bases for strenuous hill-walking; I have never been near a caravan. Pete, however, was brought up to it, travelling as a boy to France and Spain, and all round southern England; at a time when you were still allowed to park up where you wanted in wild places, and in the New Forest ponies would come and put their noses over the half-opened caravan door.

So we buy a caravan second-hand, and fit it out with extra blackout curtains (it already has good roller blinds). We join the Caravan Club. Pete goes on a Club towing course, and I read the Club magazine. I learn that a car and a caravan together are known as an "outfit"; that so-called Club sites are massive two-hundred-pitch affairs with cafés, lighting, mod cons and social activities, and sound terrifying; that small basic sites in out-of-the-way places are called Certificated Locations or CLs, and are much more what we are after; that "nose weight" and "tow weight" are vital considerations, and therefore a large number of lightweight accessories must be purchased, including aluminium pans and plastic plates.

It is important, prior to caravanning, explains Pete, to make Lists of Stuff, because it is very easy to forget something, like sharp knives or deodorant, and when you are in the middle of nowhere, this is annoying. So I pore over lists with titles like "kitchen equipment," "personal hygiene," "cultural and social activities" and "non-perishable food," and then, in the run-up to the holiday, become more and more excited, charging round the house ticking items off my lists and depositing them in the hall in special lightweight collapsible crates.

We are headed for a CL just to the west of the South Downs, about an hour's drive from home. I travel, as always, in my puppy cage, so don't see the country until we arrive. Pete has to do all the unhitching and stabilising on his own, while I sit in the car, taking peeks at trees and grass from under my felt, and itching with anticipation. Finally Pete has the caravan door open and the step down. I burst forth and leap into the van, where I busy myself unpacking stuff from under the seats and storing it in overhead lockers, then start making lunch. Pete is outside doing manly things with gas cylinders, water pipes and toilet tanks. The peculiar nature of caravanning, in combination with my medical condition, tends towards a division of labour of a highly gendered kind. I explain to Pete that, obviously, if I were in a better state of health, I would take my turn in rolling the large plastic aquahog across the field to fill it at the water tap and in carrying the toilet tank over to the pit of turds (both tasks better done in daylight), but he merely raises an eyebrow.

We picked the end of March for this holiday, because it is spring rather than winter, so hopefully not too cold, but close to the equinox, so that dawn is around 6 a.m. and dusk around 6 p.m. The later part of spring and the summer are no good, because dawn is so early and dusk so late, and in between is a very long day for me to get through, stuck in the van for hours.

Nonetheless, even in March there are early starts. The alarm clock is often set for well before dawn, so that we can drive to an interesting place and be there at first light. This is pretty knackering if repeated day after day. Luckily there is a nice wood just by the site, good for dawn walks when we can't manage to heave ourselves out of bed in the dark.

So my holiday memories are made up of a series of dusks and dawns, each one different, with its own colour and flavour. There is the dawn when we look across fields to a horizon of small lumpy hills, and beneath a flat line of grey cloud so straight that it could have been ruled with a ruler stretches an astonishing strip of tangerine sky.

There is the dusk when we climb Beacon Hill, and see in one direction Chichester Harbour and the sea, and in the other, the Hog's Back near Guildford across the furry patchwork of the Weald, and a huge bird that might have been a sparrow hawk flops down ahead of us on to the short-cropped turf, and as we come down the hill the lights come on in the valley like gold and silver beads, and a strawberry sunset glows E-number pink.

There is the dawn that starts grey and damp, stays grey and gets damper, when we walk in the woods near the caravan site, and the rain belts down all around, sizzling and hissing through the branches, blackening the bark of the trees, and only the slow brightening of the grass and moss, from grey to brilliant green, reveals that somewhere beyond the deluge, the sun is emerging above the curve of the earth.

And there is the dawn when the world is thick with frost, and our footsteps scrunch on pale shards of grass, and our flesh is flayed by the motionless blue-tinged air. We find a field which gently rises to a line of leafless trees; behind their black filigree of branches, a pastel luminescence gives a foretaste of dawn, but the sun is not yet up. In the centre of the field, a huge oak tree, perfectly proportioned, stands alone.

Pete likes the look of this tree. He gets out his camera and walks along a hedge to a gate at the corner of the field where he can get a better view.

A flock of sheep, gathered near the gate, go berserk at his approach. They rush across the frozen grass, higgledy-piggledy, towards the oak tree at the centre, and deploy themselves around it in an arrangement at once so random yet harmonious, so balanced and yet so casual, that the god of photographers (Photon?) must surely have had a hand in it. Pete takes a perfect shot.

I will always love that picture. I am so proud and pleased to have shared it with him, to be the reason why he found that field at that unholy hour, to know that the weird lifestyle that I inflict on him is not entirely inimical to Art.

On returning to the caravan, we find it is so cold that the gas bottles have frozen, which means we can't put the heater on, or make toast or cups of tea. We have cold water and bread and butter for breakfast, wearing coats, and it is not until eleven o'clock that the sun, now blazing out of a blue void, warms things enough to allow the gas to flow.

During the days, Pete and his camera go off on explorations of their own, usually coming back for lunch. I stay in the van. I read magazines and listen to music, look at maps and plan our evening excursions. I write celebratory postcards to everyone I know. "I'm on holiday!" they announce, words that people will not be expecting to hear from me, and which, for extended periods, I myself did not expect to use again.

But most of the time, I just stare out of the window. Most of the caravan's windows are kept shaded, but there is one that looks out into the feathery fronds of a cypress tree, dotted with small round cones. Sunlight dapples the foliage with twenty different shades of green, and the wind sets it dancing, and now and again a bird flies in and bounces for a while on a flexible stem.

I gaze at the rectangle of waving green, and my starved eyes revel in it and feast upon it, for hours. Even though I'm sealed in my white box, I feel the earth beneath me and the sky above me, I feel the tall trees that surround the site enfold me, and I am at peace.

Snake

Somehow, I have overdone it. Among the thousands of delicate calculations I must make each day, one has gone awry. Perhaps I stood for too long in the sunny kitchen making a chicken stir-fry, when I should simply have stuffed the beast into the oven and got out. Or perhaps I went out slightly too early at dusk or, pleased with my progress, decided to risk, on my evening constitutional, a slightly smaller hat.

It hardly matters now. Every mundane activity is a potential doorway to disaster; in the game of snakes without ladders that is my life, snakes lurk on every side. I have plunged down one; once more I am in total darkness, my skin flaming, waiting for the burning to subside. And when it does, days, weeks, perhaps months stretch out before me, while my skin slowly stabilises before I may be granted the boon of another slow climb back into the light.

The first days after a relapse are days of rage. I go over in my mind the minutiae of events that have led to my downfall, trying to pinpoint what I did wrong. I castigate myself for an over-optimistic idiot, an inattentive fool, a stupid blundering imbecile. I spool back in my mind to that fatal stir-fry or hubristic hat, and feel how easy, how simple, how trivial it would have been to have done something different. I yearn to turn back time, not to right a gross wrong, but to amend some minor mundane choice. Surely this should be allowed? It is so insignificant a thing, there could hardly be any weird or unintended consequences, any dropped stitches in the fabric of history, if I were to be permitted to have worn a different hat.

I visualise my alternative, in desperate vivid detail, paint it across my mind as I sit flaming in the darkness, see myself put on my coat and boots, reach out for my hat, open the front door, set off into the golden sunset, walk up the hill, do all that I did do but with a wider brim shading my face. Could I not by sheer force of will, by repetition, hammer this version on to the past, like a pattern hammered on to steel? But time spools resolutely forward, like the tapes, the endless tapes, of talking books to which I now return.

The stage after rage is despair. I no longer chastise myself. Instead, I feel I am accursed, that periods of progress are granted to me only so that they may be snatched away; that I am engaged upon a Sisyphean enterprise, but unlike Sisyphus, I never even reach the top of the hill, to look out, even briefly, over the universe, before my boulder crashes back down; that the task of perpetually second-guessing the whims of my skin is simply impossible, like a problem in a maths exam where there has been a misprint in the figures, and the equation, despite hours of earnest, intelligent effort, can never be solved.

I fall into a dark well. The darkness itself starts to have a horror for me—I have to force myself in and quickly slam the door. I find myself perpetually drifting out to fetch a drink, or just walk up and down the stairs. Like a bubble of air in water, or a toy duck in the bath, I have to be kept forcibly submerged.

The huge black fish called *suicide* breaks from its mud hole. Back and forth, back and forth it swims. I feel the steady beat of its fins and see with unprecedented clarity the gleam of its spiked teeth. Ten times a day tears fill my eyes, my face twists, I give a few short howls. My talking book is failing to provide the balm of distraction. Its attempted seduction seems callow and unskilful, its characters angsting about problems that are trivial in comparison to my own. To see, to smell, to move about the world before you die—these huge boons granted, why fret about the rest? I become hypersensitised to literary descriptions of nature or the weather, no matter how brief or clichéd. The opening of curtains on to a fresh crisp morning, a view of distant mountains, evening in a summer garden—all prickle me with horrible doubt: *perhaps I will not see such things again.*

In a phone call to my mother, I break down. My mother acts fast—a visit is arranged. My brother Sam will come the next day, from London. He has cancelled something he had planned that afternoon.

My brother is a gentle soul. He makes soup for our lunch. Perturbed by not finding an onion, he chops a whole head of garlic into the pot. The soup is delicious, but after a long discussion about music and politics in my dark sealed-up room, the garlicky miasma which has developed there can be cut with a knife.

BY THE FIFTH or sixth day, I have reached acceptance, slipping back into the remembered rhythm of my dark days. "See, it is not so hard," whisper my walls to me. "You have done this before."

And days, weeks, or months pass.

Games to Play in the Dark 6: Going Through the Alphabet

This is a game to play with other people or, in extremis, with yourself. Choose a category—birds, say, or colours. Then go through the alphabet and try to name an example starting with each letter. The game is collaborative rather than competitive—the pleasure lies in getting as close as possible to a full alphabetical set.

The categories are usually dictated by the interests and obsessions of the participants. With Pete, I play footballers, scientists and mathematical terms. With my brother, fictional detectives, methods of murder and world-historical figures. With my mother, operas, novelists and words that start and end with the same letter. Sometimes the category chosen proves too restrictive and a second category is added. This was the origin of "figure of speech or rude word," a memorable and entertaining round.

The Unreplenished Mind

The body starves, when nourishment stops. At first, to keep going, it turns to its reserves. It uses accumulated stores of fat for fuel. Then, as these run low, it is obliged to cannibalise more fundamental tissues. Muscles waste. Systems and processes break down. The skin becomes dry and scaly. Infections take hold. The heartbeat becomes irregular. The temperature drops.

The body eats itself.

As with a body, so with a mind. When the daily ration of fresh experience dries up, the mind turns first to its accumulated stores. For a while, it keeps functioning apparently as normal, drawing its anecdotes, points of reference and topics of conversation from its rich and many-layered reserves.

But slowly, slowly, the stock diminishes. I begin to spot the signs. I tell stories that I have told before. I speak more about my childhood, reaching further back into the store, rummaging for something new. Over and over I deploy my ten years as a working girl, so I can talk with Pete about idiotic HR departments and lunatic IT (life in large organisations does not seem to change much).

This steady drawing-down of memories causes strange disturbances within the reserves. The extraction of a single item can lead to the unexpected collapse of a whole shelving system, and the sudden surfacing of people and incidents I have not thought about for years; then they haunt my waking moments and my dreams.

Sometimes there is pleasure to be had from the fragments that float up into consciousness as the mind feeds upon its past. But my main emotion is fear. I wonder what will happen when the accumulated reserves run out. Will the mind, like the body, start to consume its own supporting structures, eat into the very sinews of consciousness? Will my clear-sightedness blur into confusion, the curve of my wit grow slack, the zip and dart of my thoughts slow to a meander, before all dissolves into mush?

What becomes of the unreplenished mind?

No one can say.

One day I talk to my brother about the time before the darkness when we took the train together on the Far North line, from Inverness to Thurso, and the train was full of Celtic fans returning from some European victory. "Don't you remember?" I ask him again and again. "We got out of the train at Thurso, and walked down the hill into the town, and it was like swimming in a river of ecstatic shiny green."

He can't recall it. I am hurt, but then remind myself that in the time since we went to the north, he has gone on many other holidays, laid down many other memories, and this one poor trip, still so vivid in my mind, is buried deep in his, several layers down.

I have to try hard to remember this, when I talk to friends and relations whose lives have not stopped.

Frogs

A story slides unexpectedly out of the bookshelves of my memory and opens itself at the front of my mind. I cannot remember where I first heard it or when— perhaps in my childhood, for it has the shape of a fable or folktale.

Something about the circumstances of my life has caused it to be brought from the archives, where it has lurked for many years, undisturbed.

Two frogs hop into the cool of a dairy on a hot day. They perch on the rims of two churns of milk, wondering whether they might have a drink. Suddenly disaster strikes—they both lose their footing and fall in. The churns are too deep and the sides are too steep for them to be able to climb out.

First Frog swims around in circles for a while. But soon he says to himself, "What is the point of all this swimming? There is no way out. I may as well stop and let myself drown, because that is what will happen eventually, in any case."

So he stops swimming, sinks to the bottom of the churn and drowns.

Meanwhile, Second Frog is swimming round in circles in the churn next door. "There does not appear to be any way out," he says to himself, "but I'm not dead yet. I'll just keep swimming round in circles as long as I can."

So he swims and he swims. "Blimey this is tedious," he thinks, as he passes a mark on the wall of the churn for the umpteenth time.

"I wonder how Bert is getting on," he thinks after a while, and shouts, "Bert! Bert!"

There is no reply from the other churn. Second Frog feels sad and alone. But he keeps on swimming.

After a long time, he says to himself wearily, "Either this milk is getting thicker or my legs are growing tired."

He keeps on swimming.

And then the milk gets very thick indeed, and Second Frog finds himself standing safely on a solid yellow surface. He hops easily out of the churn to freedom. His legs, flailing for so long, have churned the milk to butter.

The moral of the story is: Never give up.

I THINK A lot about Second Frog, as in my dark pool I struggle through the endless circling days.

Games to Play in the Dark 7: Crazy Daisy

A crazy daisy is a two-word phrase where both parts rhyme. You must also think up a "clue" for the phrase which will enable another person to guess it. The clue for "crazy daisy," for example, might be "lunatic flower."

It is not easy to come up with good crazy daisies, so even with three or four players, long pauses ensue, while everybody thinks furiously, and the heave and strain of mental machinery is practically audible.

So it is a good idea to think them up on your own, in the dark, and store them away in a pocket of your mind, for the delectation of visitors, when they come:

confused large bird	flustered bustard
mushroom-related mistake	fungal bungle
right-wing rumpus	Tory furore
ancient beverage	primordial cordial

It is always particularly satisfying when you find a rhyme for a word of unusual structure, which does not seem, at first, to be promising:

military action by small marsupial   wombat combat

Remission 2

The first thing is that I can spend a little longer out of my room. I can go from total blackness into the gloom downstairs—and stay there for a while.

The second thing is that while I am downstairs in the gloom, I can pull back one end of a long velvet curtain, and let in a feeble spindly shaft of day.

The third thing is as momentous as before. I put on my boots, my hat and coat and step into the dark garden. With great gasps, like a returning exile, I inhale the smell of the world, and walk for a while the perimeter of the lawn.

There is, once more, relief all round at the fourth thing, when I can start again to make the meals.

The fifth thing is just as risky as before, as I venture out among headlights and street lights in the night-time close.

The sixth thing involves a mirror and TV. The seventh, once again, relates to legwear. The eighth gives me, at last, a renewed glimpse of a non-dark world, painted in subtle shades of grey.

The Change

At first, every new thing is a delight. Each mundane task I add to my repertoire thrills me—no matter how tiny or trivial. "I cleaned the bathroom floor today," I announce to Pete over dinner, glowing with happy pride. In the early stages of my climb back to the light, the contrast with my previous existence is so dazzling, the flame of hope rekindled so intense, that I bubble over with high spirits. I break into impromptu dances in the kitchen, seizing my startled lover and enforcing his participation. I sing random bits of songs, some generally known, others made up on the spur of the moment to suit the circumstances. My heart is filled with gratitude and relief—gratitude that I have been granted another chance; relief that my worst fear—the fear of permanence—has yet again been proved unfounded.

And then there is a change.

It is like setting out in a boat from a dark and hideous shore, and for the first part of the journey, you look only at the place that you have left, and watch the stretch of sea between the boat and the shore steadily grow bigger, and the land recede, and you rejoice.

And then you turn your head the other way. You face the direction of travel, and you realise that the other shore is so far away that you cannot see it, but can only believe that it is there, that all around you is a blank and lonely waste of water, and that storms and monsters lie ahead.

At a certain stage of recovery—a few weeks, say, after I have re-started my dusk walks—my spirits fail me.

No longer powered by joy at what I have left behind, I see with cold detachment how far I have to go. My long and lonely days trapped in the house drag horribly; I am sick of always having to solicit visits and never going visiting; I yearn to see the inside of someone else's house—anyone's—out of sheer curiosity. A few months ago I was in ecstasy because I could leaf through a mail order catalogue. Now I am discontented because I cannot GO SHOPPING, and try on the goddamn boots *before* I have to buy. I long to make faster progress, to push my boundaries in all directions. But I know I am playing with fire.

I studied history at university. My mutinous discontent recalls something I read there on the subject of revolutions. They do not happen, it was argued, when the oppressed class is being maximally ground down by misery, but, rather, when conditions improve. It is the slight relief of pressure which gives the downtrodden the chance to lift their heads out of the slime, to look about them, and become cognisant of the true circumstances of their lives.

I try hard to count my blessings, to remind myself of the small victories I have won against the darkness, to jump upon the embers of desire.

ABC

I continue to correspond with my consultant. He is helpful in providing medical reports and letters required from time to time by some tentacle of bureaucracy, but, in terms of actual treatment, has nothing further to suggest. He would be delighted to see me if I could get to London for an appointment—but, frankly, if by my own efforts I got myself into a position where I was able to do that, I would be so delighted that I would probably carry on with whatever I had been trying, and use my new-found resilience to do something more interesting, instead.

So, like so many people who are chronically ill, I am released into the wild healthcare borderland, a trackless and confusing country, where what signposts there are point in multiple directions, sat navs fall silent, and strange beasts roam.

"Have you tried . . . ?" people say to me. "And what about . . . ?"

"Thank you for the thought," I say. "I will put it on the list."

Over the years I have tried so many things; an ABC is a more elegant method of summary than a tedious chronological account.

A IS FOR ACUPUNCTURE

"Er—I'm afraid I won't be able to take my clothes off. Would you still be prepared to treat me?"

One acupuncturist is willing to give it a go. She comes to the house and sticks needles in my hands, forearms, feet, ankles and, through my leggings, my lower legs, while explaining that, of course, this limited approach is sub-optimal. I persist for eight sessions, but there is no discernible effect.

B IS FOR BREATHING

"Breathing incorrectly is the root cause of a huge variety of chronic health conditions. Retrain your breathing using these revolutionary new techniques and join thousands of people worldwide who have recovered health and well-being through following the unique approach developed by Dr. Randall P. Whitebait . . ."

Aha! Breathing!

Now there is something a person can do in the dark. I accept my friend's offer of a set of Breathing CDs and a workbook.

Some of the exercises make me feel pleasantly relaxed. Others put my back out. On the light sensitivity they have no discernible effect.

C IS FOR CHELATION

My friend Tom, advocate of the empowering qualities of the Web, does a lot of detailed health research online. He finds a community of people with a range of chronic conditions who have achieved major improvements in their health by reducing high levels of mercury in their bodies. A test can determine if mercury toxicity might be a problem—some people are genetically more able to get rid of it naturally than others.

According to the results, Tom and I both have a mercury problem. We start taking a sulphur compound which binds to the mercury (chelates it) and enables it to be peed out of the body.

I enjoy four months of amazing, cumulative, measurable improvement.

Then I have a horrible relapse. My total light sensitivity returns, and I am completely exhausted. It appears that chelation puts a strain on the adrenal glands, and mine are very weak.

I try chelating several more times, but the results are always the same: shaking, sweating, collapse.

Tom fares much better. He persists with chelation over four years, and becomes well enough to start another business—this time, doing computer modelling for eco-homes.

D IS FOR DIET

One New Year's Eve, feeling rather fine, I eat eight chocolates one after the other on an empty stomach, while drinking champagne.

Next day, I start the New Year with a truly horrible relapse. I can't even come out of the black to watch the New Year's Day concert live from Vienna and dance to the "Blue Danube" waltz, which has become a tradition in our household.

Intrigued, I investigate the physiological effects of spikes in blood sugar, and discover the low GI diet (GI stands for glycaemic index, which is a measure of how fast a particular food is converted into glucose by the body). I give up alcohol, sugar and refined carbohydrates, and combine protein and carbs at each meal. It definitely helps.

E *IS FOR ENERGY HEALING*

A plummy voice on the answerphone:

"This is Venetia Winstanley speaking. I have been treating your hair in my machine for the last few days, and I am telephoning to establish whether there has been any improvement."

What? What?! Who is this woman, and how has she got hold of my hair? And given I've been feeling pretty terrible for the last few days, whatever she is doing, I would like to ask her to stop.

Eventually the whole thing is untangled. Venetia Winstanley is some sort of distance energy healer, who once saved the life of a child of a friend of my mother's. The friend persuaded my mother to send this character some of my hair, which she did several months ago, having snipped a few strands from the back of my head. A death in the healer's family delayed further action until now; the hair had completely slipped my mind.

F *IS FOR FATTY ACIDS*

A blood test shows something in the way I process essential fatty acids is definitely out of whack. A nutritionist recommends a particular supplement, emulsified to make the EFAs easier to absorb. I improve steadily for four months.

Then the manufacturer stops making the supplement. Nothing else on the market has the same effect.

G IS FOR GROUNDING

According to the blurb on my Grounding book, sickness, pain and inflammation are the result of being Electron Deficient, and can be helped by Nature's own anti-inflammatory—the Earth itself!

Ideally, you ground yourself by walking about barefoot on grass or soil and by sleeping directly on the ground. If this is not feasible, you can purchase a grounding bedsheet—a cotton sheet incorporating a conductive mesh of metal wires, which is then attached by a thicker wire to a grounding rod stuck into the earth outside.

I think I must have had some sort of allergic reaction to lying on metal. After two nights, my skin is puffy, my heart is racing, and I have a horrible relapse.

H IS FOR HYPNOTHERAPY

"The skin all over your body is calm and cool," intones the CD made for me by the hypnotherapist. "You continue to become even more deeply relaxed."

I lie in the dark and listen to the smooth, soothing voice. My skin, unfortunately, does not.

I IS FOR INK

I expend a lot of ink writing to private doctors who specialise in the holistic treatment of allergies and environmental sensitivities. I offer large sums of money to entice them into a home visit or a telephone consultation. Most of them will not treat anyone who cannot attend their clinic.

J IS FOR JUMPING UP AND DOWN

I have a small trampoline, known as a rebounder. According to the accompanying book, rebounding is a superior form of exercise, which can have life-changing effects on a whole range of chronic conditions.

I look forward to my daily half-hour of jumping up and down. It does not cure me, but it certainly cheers me up.

K IS FOR KINESIOLOGY

Ask the body questions—and actually get answers!

Hold out your arm, and let the therapist try to push it down. Sometimes the arm is strong and sometimes it is weak, and from this, guidance and conclusions can be drawn.

For me, whose body has become an unfathomable mystery, this promise is incredibly, overwhelmingly seductive—and for the first few treatments, during which the therapist recommends certain supplements, I improve markedly. But eventually, I lose my faith. Things that, according to the muscle testing, should be good for my body provoke nasty reactions. And other things, which I know help, come up with negative results. It is hard to persist, once basic faith has gone.

L *IS FOR LOGBOOK*

I write down everything that I try and how I feel. I log it in my logbook, a page-per-day diary. I monitor the data in my logbook for trends, hungry for cause and effect. But there are so many variables—it is like playing multi-dimensional chess, an easy route to madness.

M *IS FOR MEDITATION*

It seems strange to create an oasis of nothingness within a life that is already too full of nothing. What I crave is busyness, purpose and stimulation—but nonetheless I try meditating, having read about its possible benefits to health.

CDs that invite me to imagine myself in a beautiful garden or floating above sunlit clouds distress rather than soothe me. I do better with techniques that involve simply focusing on the breath, observing it as it flows in and out. Sometimes I try counting the breaths down from ten to one, but my mind often wanders, getting lost somewhere between seven and six, and I have to start over again.

There is no appreciable effect on the light sensitivity—but I find that this technique does calm me, bringing me back to the present moment when, prompted by some news item about breast cancer or stroke, I think too much about the future, panic about the risk-beset fragility of my existence, foresee a hundred painful ways that I could die.

N IS FOR NUTS

On my low GI diet, I eat a lot of nuts.

O IS FOR OPEN-MINDED

As an anonymous Scotsman once said to the composer Sir Arnold Bax: "Try everything once, except for incest and folk-dancing."

Indeed.

P IS FOR PRAYER

Sometimes people tell me that they are praying for me. I feel immensely moved and grateful. Although I cannot travel physically, it is encouraging to think that, in distant churches and cathedrals, I am nonetheless strangely present, at least in someone's mind, and in their heart.

Q IS FOR QUEST

It is better to travel hopefully than to arrive and know that hope has gone. So long as there is a road ahead of me, so long as there are things on my list still left to try, I am cushioned against despair. Even as each episode proves fruitless, I have learned something, each time, by my own efforts, if only that another possibility can be eliminated, and I can now move on to the next.

R IS FOR RATIONALITY

I wonder what a committed scientific rationalist would do, were he to find himself in my predicament. Here, there are no randomised controlled trials, and science itself is silent.

I would like to be researched. The one thing that surprises me is that no one has wanted to take a biopsy of my skin. Where is their scientific curiosity? I am sure the results would be interesting.

S IS FOR SPIRITUAL HEALING

After my third session, I tell the spiritual healer that I am very grateful for all her efforts, but I am not feeling any positive effects, and therefore do not think it is worth carrying on.

She gazes into my eyes. "I sense that you have some deep psychological wound," she says, "which is causing you subconsciously to resist the healing energy, and you will not get better until you have worked through your deep emotional trauma."

I could headbutt her, but I do not. Instead, overwhelmed by glorious, transcendent absurdity, I burst out laughing, and keep laughing as I escort her to the door.

T IS FOR TESTS

I have a lot of tests. They are recommended by private doctors and other practitioners and carried out by private laboratories. I get to know the home-visiting phlebotomist, a cheery lady who operates under the title "The Scottish Vampire," and who tightens around my arm a strap decorated with Dracula cartoons. Pete takes packages containing a range of bodily fluids to the post office; he gradually becomes inured to filling out embarrassing declarations about their contents.

U is for upshot

The upshot of all these tests is that vast swathes of me (amazingly, given how I have been living) are working well. The exceptions are my metabolism of essential fatty acids, which is "deranged," my methylation cycle (something to do with the liver) and my adrenal glands, which are so useless at producing cortisol that by rights I ought to be clinically dead.

But are these anomalies causes or consequences of my sensitivity to light? And will the huge lists of supplements recommended to treat them actually be absorbed and tolerated by my system? I find I do feel somewhat better if I take stuff to support my adrenal glands, and that eating foods rich in essential fatty acids like pumpkin seeds, flax seeds and grass-fed steak has a noticeable soothing effect on the skin, but the vitamins recommended to promote methylation, and most oily supplements, make things worse.

One private doctor, impressed by my poor adrenal function, recommends, in addition to supplements, a low-dose steroid, hydrocortisone, and for a couple of months I experience significant improvement. Then, on upping the dose as instructed, the improvement goes into sharp and nasty reverse, and I am back mostly in the black, not venturing beyond the night-time garden. I want to stop taking the things but of course I cannot, now being dependent; any reduction will have to be done very slowly and carefully, with excitingly weird side effects, and no guarantee of success.

So I have some peripheral pieces for my jigsaw, but in the centre, there is still empty space.

V IS FOR VISUALISATION

"My adult student Elizabeth," says my mother, "had a hole in her retina, and was on a waiting list for an operation, and she visualised the hole closing up every day for three months, and when she went in for the operation, they could no longer find the hole."

"Hmmm," I say, "I suppose it's worth a go. What should I be visualising, do you think?"

"Er . . . what about—the curtain gradually opening?"

"But then—if the technique actually works—all that might happen is the curtain might gradually open, and that would be no use at all."

"Good point."

In the end I decide to visualise putting on an all-over protective body suit, like a second skin, and do this religiously every morning.

Not much happens.

W *IS FOR WEIRDEST*

THE ENERGY EGG (ACCORDING TO ITS WEBSITE)

- eliminates accumulated environmental stress

- protects human life energies from all forms of sha chi

- provides full body protection, including from other people's energies

- does not emit any harmful energies itself

- updates itself manually or automatically

My energy egg is about three centimetres high. It is indeed egg-shaped, made of polished white stone, cool to the touch. According to the instructions, it must be kept within one centimetre of the body, so I carry it about in my pocket for several months.

In the end, I conclude that I feel better without it, as it contributes to a slight lopsided tendency, which is not good for my back.

X *IS FOR XPERIMENTS*

In the absence of anyone knowing what to do about my condition, the only way forward is to experiment. But being the sole subject of my own experiments is frustrating and inefficient; every experiment has the potential to make me worse as well as better, and given the general fluctuation it can be hard to disentangle the results.

I dream of having a library of clones—six versions of me, made specially meek and compliant, kept boxed up in a cupboard when not in use, and brought out to eat strange pills and trial peculiar devices, as required.

This is not an uncommon fantasy, I find, among the chronically ill.

Y IS FOR YAWN, Z IS FOR ZZZZ

Goodness it is boring having to keep thinking about my health. Every so often I become completely fed up with the whole business and have to take a break, simply to be.

ON THE WHOLE, Pete supports my experiments, and tolerates the more outlandish ones. Kinesiology, however, is where he draws the line. Part of the treatment involves attempting gradually to desensitise the body to a range of substances, in order to reduce its total allergic load. After a session in which I am desensitised to, for example, sugars, I am instructed to keep at least four feet away from any items which contain them for the next twenty-five hours. To assist me, the kinesiologist helpfully places the biscuits in a cupboard, the bread in a corner under the boiler and the fruit bowl in the office upstairs.

When Pete comes in from work he goes quietly berserk.

"That woman's been here, hasn't she?" he growls, prowling round the kitchen. "It's bloody bananas in the washing machine again. And where's the bread? Can you give me a clue? I want to make some toast."

Terror

Terror comes at me out of a clear sky, slamming me into the ground.

Half a page in a local council magazine. Money available under the Private Finance Initiative to replace street lights in the county more than fifteen years old. A consultation exercise to be held, so that people may make their views known. In place of traditional sodium lamps, the council is considering bright white fluorescent "daylight" lighting.

If they install white lights, I will never be able to leave the house.

If they install white lights behind my back fence, I will never be able to use my garden.

At first, I am too shocked to do anything, too shocked, even, to work out what action I should take. The impending beams transfix me; I can only sit and stare at my approaching doom.

But after a couple of days, my mental paralysis starts to abate. Stuck cogs shift, small flickerings of electric pulses dart across neural circuits. Avenues that might be worth exploring occur to me; an occasional sentence for a possible letter drafts itself randomly in my head.

I want to know the council's freedom of manoeuvre. Is it their choice to install white lights, or are they being directed by a higher power? I write to the Department of Transport, and receive a reply saying that the EU Street Lighting Directive (of course! How could I have possibly imagined that street lighting might be a matter of national sovereignty?) requires only that old-fashioned low-pressure sodium lamps be changed, when they come to be replaced, to more energy-efficient high-pressure sodium lamps, and does not mandate the move to white fluorescent. Local councils should take account of local factors, says the DoT.

I write a response to the consultation. I receive a letter from the council. It says, "Thank you for highlighting your concerns about the impact of white light on people with light-sensitivity conditions. I have received many helpful and constructive ideas for future street-lighting provision. Please be assured that these will all be considered before any firm decision is taken."

The letter, with its careful, non-committal wording, makes me positively nostalgic. "Highlighting your concerns about the impact of" rather than "explaining the difficulties caused by" is quite masterly—in other words, you say there's a problem, we don't have to believe you. I am all too familiar with what is going on—it's what, in a slightly different context, I used to do for a living when I walked the corridors of power, a handmaiden of the elect. I wrote "lines to take" to help ministers answer difficult questions. And I formulated standard paragraphs for use by correspondence units in replying to letters from the public, such as my own.

Some time after the end of the council's consultation exercise, I have heard nothing about the outcome, and am getting jumpy. I know too well the desire of the bureaucrat for things to progress smoothly. I, if I had received my own letter, would have simply placed it in a sort of holding pen for the peculiar, and pressed on regardless, unless something more dramatic occurred.

I write to my local councillor, for help in finding out what is going on. The councillor acts fast and constructively, contacting the street lighting project and asking them to talk to me. They send, in the first instance, a communications manager. She is an enthusiastic, well-dressed young lady, who tells me how wonderful the new street lights will be. They'll be just like daylight, so colours will look the same as in sunshine, and the police will be more easily able to identify a thug wearing, for example, a purple hoodie. They will be angled downwards, rather than outwards, so there will be less light pollution, which will be better for astronomers. They will be remote-controlled, so that the council can dim them after midnight, in genteel neighbourhoods where crime is low.

I listen to all of this, then explain patiently that, unfortunately, these features do not address my problem, which is, if these lamps are installed in my area, I will no longer be able to leave the house. I ask if a final decision in favour of these lamps has been made. Sheepishly, the communications manager admits that it has.

I suspected as much. Yet to have it confirmed is as if this pleasant, smartly suited young lady has taken, from her chic leather bag, a slim pistol, and, as we sit opposite each other in armchairs in my own living room, has shot me in the guts.

I know I must come back fighting. Luckily, I've done my homework. I have obtained a guide to the Disability Discrimination Act, which makes clear that it covers local authorities and public spaces, of which the streets would seem to be a prime example. Service providers are required to make reasonable adjustments to enable a disabled person to have access. I say that I'm not asking for access to the whole of the county or even my own town—but simply for an area around my house to be left with sodium street lights, so that I can continue to have a daily walk. I show the lady spectrum diagrams of different types of lighting, including a graph of the make-up of daylight itself. I explain that light at the blue end of the spectrum is higher frequency, and therefore more damaging to light-sensitive people, and that white "daylight" lighting contains a much greater proportion of these more energetic, "bluer" wavelengths.

The lady listens to my theory lesson. She questions how I can know the new lamps will be a problem, when they haven't been installed yet. I do, sadly, know this—a couple have been put up at the end of one of the closes I visit in my daily dusk walk, to shed extra light on a footpath. I walked past them as an experiment, buoyed by irrational hope; the following night was agony.

The communications manager says she will pass on

the content of our conversation, but can make no commitments. She leaves.

The next few months are horrible. Hearing nothing from the project, I have to do what I hate, having been brought up to show consideration for others, and not to make a fuss. I have to hassle people, phone up, leave messages, copy emails to my councillor. Every time my assistant logs on to my emails, my heart pounds, in case, lurking in my inbox, is a communication affecting my fate. When there's once again nothing, I feel a surge of guilty relief. But later, I am in a quandary again, trying to decide whether I should make another phone call, or wait another week. Am I jeopardising my case by over-prosecution, or is there some invisible clock on which my time is ticking away?

When I psych myself up to telephone, I am trembling, and afterwards must take several deep breaths and lie down.

My interlocutors know nothing of all this. My emails are always polite and professional. On the telephone I sound friendly and hyper-rational, but not as if I am going to go away. I know I cannot afford, even once, to lose control; to allow the emotions roiling below the surface to bubble up would risk being labelled as a madwoman, a neurotic, a person no longer to be listened to but to be *handled*, a person who has ceased to be an equal.

The dilemma must be familiar to everyone who finds, suddenly, by some weird sleight of circumstance, that they must engage with the State. The State is the power that can do unto you, without asking your leave, the power that can grant or withhold, the power whose favour can only ever be solicited, and never be demanded.

They will not believe there is a problem, if you allow too little distress to show. Allow too much, and you're officially a nutter.

My own father, a mild and considerate cello player, went several times to his doctor over a period of years, because he had headaches that were becoming more frequent, and growing difficulty moving the fingers of his left hand. The doctor told him, each time, that he was suffering from stress. He collapsed on a concert tour of Germany, walking along a footpath beside the Rhine, with a brain tumour that had grown large enough to paralyse him down the left side. Sixteen months later he was dead.

I pace the streets of my neighbourhood on my dusk walks. I breathe in the smell of damp gardens, old leaves, seasonal blossoms, the vapour of hot days, the scent of the wind. I watch the daily show of the sunset upon the screen of the sky as it creates its never-repeated pattern of cloud and dying light. I try to tell myself: enjoy it now, enjoy it today, don't think about a future when this is closed to you, when if you want to walk you'll be dependent on others, boxed up and transported to somewhere unlit and out of the way.

I wonder what self-help advice is given to those under sentence of death, as they await the outcome of their last appeals. Would an extreme proponent of positive thinking recommend not even contemplating the possibility of failure in case this opens the door to the reality? I feel I have to give some time to mental trial runs, so that the shock, if it must come, will be less catastrophic, because I have already been through it, in my mind.

Eventually I receive an email saying that the communications manager has left the project, and that any contact should now be with the project director.

I engage with the project director. Sensibly, he asks if I can obtain a letter from my consultant about the white light problem, which I do. After several months I have a general reassurance from the project director that they won't install street lights "in the immediate vicinity of my home" that will be "injurious to my health."

I know from my previous life how slippery words can be. I know that what looks, on first reading, like a commitment, can actually, when it comes to the crunch, be nothing of the sort. It's no reflection on the integrity of the individuals involved; they are simply part of a system addicted to wiggle room. But the net result of my ten years in Whitehall is I'm wary of anyone or anything official. So I'm concerned to get detailed specifics on the council's plans, and in a form more formal than an email.

After another few months of phone calls and emails, I learn that the project director has left the project. I ask my local councillor again for help. After a few weeks, I am contacted by a senior engineer, who comes to visit me, with a map.

He says white fluorescent lighting is not suitable everywhere anyway, and he would like me to indicate where I walk on the map, so that a special area of sodium lamps can be installed (they still want to replace the lamps themselves), rather like a nature reserve for an exotic, endangered species. He can't guarantee everything I ask for, but will aim for some of it.

At these signs of intelligence and humanity, I almost collapse with relief. I want to embrace this grey-haired, soft-spoken man, my low-key, geeky saviour.

I submit my annotated map, but then, for several months, hear nothing definite except that they are very busy sorting out the contract. I wonder if the sensible engineer has been overruled by some other, less amenable, part of the bureaucracy. I'm worried that I'm still relying on personal assurances from a project whose implementation dates are growing closer, and whose staff have a marked tendency to leave.

It's two years since the consultation exercise. The long period of uncertainty, in tandem with the constant effort to overcome my natural instincts and keep hassling, has slowly drained me. I have read books on how to manage stress, have learned how to breathe through my feet, to breathe in for four and out for nine, to breathe so that my belly rises and falls, to meditate by focusing on the breath. But I still feel like crumpled paper. I decide it's time to bring things to a head.

I email the local law firms, and pick the one which gives the sole intelligent response. A fierce and rigorous partner comes to see me, asks a lot of questions and takes away a lot of papers. She drafts a letter which makes references to the Disability Discrimination Act, the Disability Equality Duty, and the Human Rights Act.

But in the end, the letter is not sent. I start putting the solicitor on the copy list of my emails and mention I have consulted one. A plan of my area arrives from the council. It shows the position, reference number and type of every street light. The streets and footpaths around my house are edged with a glorious golden glow. The accompanying email says, furthermore, that the rollout of new lamps in my neighbourhood will be scheduled at the end of the implementation period, so it won't happen for a couple of years, at least.

I am dizzy with relief. I allow myself, even, some modest jubilation. But my past training still does not desert me. I put all the papers in a file, tell the solicitor to retain my set, and wait to see if promises will be kept.

Wedding

During a long and hopeful period of remission in 2007, Pete and I decide to have another go at a wedding. With a light-sensitive bride, the whole event has to be reconfigured. We consult the sunset times in my diary and find that on 6 December the sun will set at 15:57. So we decide we will get married on that day, at four o'clock.

It is no longer feasible to hold the ceremony and reception in a hotel. I need to be able to control the amount and type of lighting in my environment, and to retreat periodically to my lair. Pete investigates the registry office in town; it is a nightmare of ferocious strip lights and large plate glass windows.

But the church where we were going to have a blessing is still suitable. It is very old, and the village that once surrounded it moved in the Middle Ages because of plague. So it now stands in the middle of fields, with few surrounding lights. Inside, it is lit by a series of sodium spots, high up in the beams of the roof.

The church is one to which Pete has belonged for many years. When he first arrived in the area, he investigated the surrounding Church of England establishments to find one in which he would feel at home—in the expression used by those in the know, neither too low down nor too high up the candle. He eschewed the church nearest to his house, a barn of glass and yellow brick and fluorescent lighting, where the words of praise songs descend from the ceiling on screens and the congregation wave their arms unencumbered by hymn books.

My own religious background is more complex. My mother is Jewish (Reform rather than Orthodox); my father, originally a Scottish Presbyterian, passed through both Marxist and New Age phases before converting to Catholicism two years before his death. Growing up, I never felt fully immersed in either camp, and although occasionally I envied the coherent community life of my cousins, I also enjoyed being able to step back, observe from outside, and develop my own perspective. I had never envisaged having a church wedding, but the logic of our situation is becoming inescapable. If we want to get married, it looks like we are going to have to do it in the church. It takes me a while to come to terms with this, but finally, I admit it to Pete. "But will they have me?" I wonder. We write to the vicar explaining the position, and I am pleased when I find out that the Church of England, as an established church, considers that it has the care of all souls within the land, including mine, and will marry me even though I am not a Christian. I am even allowed to omit "through Jesus Christ our Lord" when I say my vows. It is all most sensible and civilised.

I have a wedding dress. It is bluebell–blue satin, with embroidered flowers climbing up from the hem. But wearing the dress alone is not an option any more. The dressmaker sews a fitted jacket, in matching material, and well lined, for me to wear over the top.

I also need a hat. I decide to work on the principle that if one has to wear a hat to one's own wedding, it might as well be a humdinger. I find in the Yellow Pages a character called "The Mad Hatter," who is prepared to come to the house. Together we concoct a millinerial event—bluebell blue, with an enormous brim, and a vast silk flower.

It is a splendid creation. The only disadvantage, as Pete and I will discover on the day, is that the brim is so wide that it discourages intimacy. We can't stand too close together for the wedding pictures, or the groom gets hit in the face.

The reception is to be reduced in size and relocated to the house. The house is not a large one, so we plan to get extra floor space by hiring a marquee which will attach on to the back of the conservatory, and fill up nearly the whole garden. The guests will be kept warm by gas heaters and energetic Scottish dancing. There will be a bar in the bay window at the front end of the living room, and food set out on tables in the conservatory, for guests to help themselves.

Five weeks before the wedding I step on a snake.

It is a long one.

I have had months of slow but uninterrupted improvement. I have reached f22 on my light meter—meaning that I can go out about an hour before sunset, and stay out for the same time after dawn.

I have begun to teach the piano to local children, putting into practice, at last, what I learnt on my course. There seems to be a demand—soon I have eleven pupils, and am planning to hold an informal concert for parents and friends, to be followed by a tea party involving lots of cake.

The teaching is my undoing. My pupils come in the after-school slot, two or three most weekdays. I have been used to teaching the first two by natural daylight, and only putting the piano lamp on for the third.

At the end of October the clocks go back and the evenings become darker. I teach three pupils in succession under the glare of the piano lamp.

It is too much.

For the whole of the following night I feel as though cheese graters are being slowly pulled across my body. The next day, I can hardly leave my dark room.

TWO WEEKS BEFORE the wedding, my state has not shown much improvement. Pete and I debate what to do—to cancel the wedding for a second time, or to plough on regardless.

In the end we decide to carry on. Standing in the living room I make a statement to Pete, looking into his eyes, holding on to his elbows so that he cannot turn away. I tell him that if, subsequent to the wedding, my condition does not improve, I will understand if he decides to divorce me.

"OK," he replies. "But let's hope it doesn't come to that."

We wrap our arms around each other and kiss for a long time.

This is my true wedding vow, my dark vow, the one that will, if I have to keep it, shred my heart. The promises I will make on the day are easy and obvious; with my dark vow I make obeisance to the forces that shift implacably within the black pit of life, that twist and break the finest, strongest things. In ninety-nine out of a hundred possible worlds, we are ideal companions; this may be the one in which we're not.

The final two weeks pass in some sort of surrealist nightmare. I spend as much time as possible in the dark, trying to stabilise my skin, popping up to take delivery of my hat, try on my jacket, speak on the phone about the cake (I can hardly remember what it is supposed to look like). All sorts of things that I had once thought important fall by the wayside. I am given a silly haircut by a visiting hairdresser, who refuses to come back and fix it; I can't cope with the hassle of finding anybody else.

The day before the wedding, I sit upstairs in my room while a rumpus goes on underneath. Men charge in and out installing the marquee, demanding that bits be cut off various trees and shrubs so that it will fit. Friends arrive to help shift furniture. The flower lady turns up in a car full of greenery and blossoms, blue, pink and white, and starts installing her arrangements. Pete comes in to give me periodic reports and show me photographs of the more interesting developments. In between these, I listen to my talking book. It's *Bravo Two Zero*.

And it's *Bravo Two Zero* the next day as well. I am glad, because the story of an SAS patrol stuck behind enemy lines in the first Gulf War is at least gripping and true. It helps me to forget that this is my wedding day, that it has not turned out as I had expected, that I do not know what will happen in the afternoon, when I put on my outfit and go to the church, whether I will be able to stand it, even with most of the lights off, how much pain there is to come.

During the morning of my wedding day, the narrator is captured by Iraqi soldiers. He is beaten up, taken for interrogation, beaten up, displayed to an angry mob, convinced he is about to be shot or torn to pieces, beaten up again.

Suddenly it's three o'clock. I turn off the torture

scenes. Hurriedly, I put on my dress and jacket. I take several beta carotene tablets, which can sometimes take the edge off my reactions. In the unlit bathroom, peering into the mirror at my dim reflection, I hazard a small amount of make-up, and put on my hat. When I come downstairs, Pete opens the front door of the house and the back door of the car. A few desultory raindrops spatter the close from a mottled grey sky, but on the horizon, gaps in the cloud reveal pale primrose patches of light. I dash across the two-metre gap and dive inside my puppy cage, while trying to preserve the upstandingness of my silk flower.

"Right," says Pete. "Are you in?"

I thrash about, fastening my seatbelt, and shifting the recalcitrant folds of felt so that they press less heavily on my head, but still provide protection around the legs and feet.

"I'm ready," I say. "I hope it's not going to pour down. Let's go for it!"

He starts up the engine, and we move off into the uncertain December dusk.

In the end, adrenaline and absurdity get me through. My memories are an agglomeration of intense, mad, joyful fragments, like a web of fairy lights: walking up the aisle with Pete to "Wachet auf" by Bach; the weird lighting in the church, where most of the central lights are off, but the ones at the sides are on, and there are huge white candles at the altar, and smaller ones in stone niches and on windowsills; nearly fainting when

I come to say my vows, suddenly overwhelmed by the realisation that we've made it this far; at the party afterwards, whirling triumphantly up and down the marquee, flung from partner to partner, as we collectively work out, finally, how to "strip the willow"; my stepmother, on the waiting list for a hip operation, throwing aside her walking sticks and joining in; a young girl on the trampoline in the children's corner, daughter of one of Pete's colleagues, bouncing, bouncing, blonde hair flying; the sudden onset, halfway through, of anxiety about loo rolls (there are seventy people in the house), and Pam driving valiantly to Tesco to bring back an enormous multipack.

I remember the man we hired to call the dancing, huge, impossibly extrovert, looking like a portrait of Henry VIII; my mother, in brown velvet, sitting down at the piano and busking Scottish songs. I remember discovering, at the end of the evening, that I have been so busy talking to people that I have hardly eaten any food (two olives and a potato) and therefore have no idea whether, after all our care with caterers, it was any good; retreating upstairs twice, with some select companions, to rest my skin and chat for a while in the blackness; the spicy smell of pink lilies, as, in the heat of bodies, they slowly unfurled their long-lipped blooms, and pumped their perfume into every part of the house.

The Eternal Return

I continue to lurch a little way up the hill of recovery, and then roll down to the bottom again. I might reach stage five, or stage three, or stage ten, before a snake slips under my foot, and I lose all the ground that I have gained. Plans made in hope during an upward trajectory become, by the date they should come to fruition, mere absurdities; it is hard to believe that they once seemed within my grasp.

Three times I arrange to go to Stonehenge at dawn, a most suitable trip for a light-sensitive person, when one can pay to be let in and walk among the stones. There is always high demand, and booking is required several months ahead, plus the completion of an application form requiring details of "musical instruments" and "any ceremony that will be performed." But each time the date arrives, everything has changed, my skin is flaming, the trip impossible; things are always being cancelled and dismantled—caravan sites unbooked, guests disinvited, concert tickets left unused.

I should become inured. But I do not.

I lose whole seasons, and sometimes more than seasons. One year I leave the world in March, icy winds whipping the daffodils, and come into it again in the sullen heat of June. The next, I water the garden on an evening in May, inhaling the sweetness of lilac and the sour tang of hawthorn, sensing in everything the bubbling expectancy of summer. I will not stir outside again until the leaves are turning, and all the exuberance rots on the compost heap or hangs limply from shrivelled stems. It is as if I open a secret door in time, wander into a dark side passage, and am unable to find an exit. I grope my way forward, not knowing how far I have to go, until suddenly my fingers close on a handle set into the wall, a door opens, and I find myself on the main route again, but a long way further on.

When I look back, these blocks of time are blanked out in my mind, scored through with a thick black marker as if my memories were documents redacted by some conscientious official. But it's not true to say I retain nothing from these periods of abeyance. From that lost summer, roses and apples make up my memories. The roses were cut for me by Pete, and glowed darkly in the curtained living room, scenting the shadowy air. I would lift the vases to my face, and press my nose to the velvety depths, and breathe and breathe, as if each flower were the mouth of a pipe connecting me to the world. The apples piled up in boxes on the kitchen floor, enormous, shining, warm from the sun, astonishingly perfect, endless. I would go into the kitchen, just to gaze. They seemed an unasked-for, slightly inconvenient miracle, performed on the apple tree by a passing angel in randomly benevolent mood, unaware of the girl inside the house, who would have liked a miracle for herself.

Pete shows me photos during these dark times, a procession of shining images on a tiny screen. He collects them in the world outside, fixes them in his camera like bright butterflies, lays his haul before me, to show what he has seen.

This is how he shares with me the landscapes that

we loved, together, in the life before. He connects me, through the pictures, to his travels, keeps me in some way with him as he wanders through the world.

Blue skies over fields pocked with haystacks; a hurly-burly of poppies; sun-dappled green.

Low light on autumn beeches; red leaves in water; a fungus like fine china on a shaggy tablecloth of moss.

Through them I know the rhythm of the seasons, the alteration of the quality of light, as the sun arcs high and steep towards midsummer then drops down to the low rays of the turn of the year. Through them I see the different plants come into leaf and flower and fruit, each in their time; I see the trees blaze in glory and then burn away to stiff black fingers poking at sullen skies.

A frosted birch on a path that leads into mist. Swirl patterns in the ice over a pond. Five slender trees in snow, dancing.

Snowdrops in profusion beside dark water. A single daffodil, snowy and surprised. Multi-coloured primroses, advancing.

Time Bends

I am in the garden with my oldest friend, hitting a tumbling shuttlecock high, high up into a lilac-blue sky. It is the evening of a breathless day, the sun just poised above the horizon, the last rays slipping between long shadows to set patches of foliage ablaze. On one side the game is hemmed in by the pots on the patio, on the other by the straggling branches of the cherry tree. There is no net—it's exhilarating enough to keep up a rally, to feel the satisfying "thwunk" as the shuttlecock's rubbery nose connects with the centre of the racket strings.

My friend is wearing sandals and a summer dress. I am wearing a straw hat, a tailored jacket, a long-sleeved T-shirt, a long skirt, leggings, socks and lace-up boots. My body temperature is rising steadily. Sweat trickles down my neck and back. Each time I move, fabrics clutch my flesh like damp unwelcome hands. But I don't care. I'm outside, I'm free, I'm moving about on the surface of the earth.

I clip the shuttlecock with the edge of my racket, and it zips off sideways. "Bother, I can't do backhands," I say. "I think it went into this bush." I delve among the cool green stems, inhaling the moist fragrance of the soil, until I find a flash of white. I serve to start the next rally, and my friend hits a soaring return—but then, lunging for the place where the shuttlecock should be, my racket sweeps only empty, heavy air. The highest branch of the cherry tree, reaching over the lawn like a hairy admonitory arm, has grabbed the shuttlecock at the top of its flight path, and held it fast.

"Oh flamers," says my friend. "It's stuck."

The two of us approach the tree. We grasp the rough divided trunks and shake them hard. Leaves and bits of twig fall from the tree on to our heads. A perturbed bird scoots out to one side and settles on the fence. The shuttlecock stays on its high perch.

"We could try throwing a racket at it," I suggest.

"That'll probably get stuck too," my friend replies.

And suddenly time bends, and the years fold back upon themselves, and I am ten years old again, and my friend is nine, and we are in another garden in another time, barefoot among the daisies, looking upwards into a different tree and laughing. Three shuttlecocks and two rackets are held captive high inside its intricate canopy, completely out of reach.

My thoughts reach out to the child that I was, far away on the other side of the darkness, innocent of my future, full of loopy hopes and dreams. I am overwhelmed by a ferocious sense of continuity, a pull through my solar plexus as though I were attached to a giant anchor chain. Beneath the deformations of solitude, the dents left by acute despair, the slimy residue of chronic fear (of painful death, of dissolution, of the unravelling of my mind), beneath all the accretions of suffering, I am still that self, the core of me unchanged. And my friend, whose memories entwine with mine, stands alongside me, my witness and my proof.

I step away from the tree. With one hand to my hat to hold it on my head, I lean back to calculate my aim. Then I hurl my racket into the sultry air. Head over handle it turns as it soars, a final sunbeam catching the silver frame and making it flash fire. The racket crashes into the straggling branch, and the shuttlecock springs free. Both hang for a moment in the lilac sky, an outline moon and a feathery star, before they plunge to earth.

Unexpected

"I found something unexpected in the garden this afternoon," Pete says over dinner one Saturday evening. He has been cutting the grass, and taking annuals out of pots, and doing other end-of-summer tasks.

"Goodness," I say. "What was that? Was it a wild boar?"

"No, not one of those. I know you'd like it to be, darling, but it wasn't."

"A frog then." Our garden backs on to the little valley with the stream; frogs occasionally hop in.

"No. Look, stop trying to guess, because you won't. It's the yucca plant. It's producing a flower."

"A flower?"

"A whacking great protuberance that's already about five feet high."

"How extraordinary—but that yucca . . ."

"Hasn't done anything since I bought the house, and that was twenty years ago."

Indeed, the yucca has always struck me as a tiresome, unlovely plant, squatting too close to the path from the back door like a pair of spiky malevolent pompoms, and periodically having to be cut back with scissors to stop it skewering people's thighs. Recently, we had discussed digging it out, but concluded that this would be very difficult, and require protective clothing.

I am less well than I was earlier in the summer;

we have to wait until well after sunset before I can go outside. Pete points out the nascent flower spike; it is thicker than my wrist, carbuncled with bulges, and with a thrusting, pointed head.

"That's obscene," I say. "How did it get that big without us noticing?"

"They sort of sneak up on you," says Pete.

"It's positively sinister."

And each day, when I venture into the garden at the grey end of dusk, the thing seems to have grown another couple of inches, and is developing side shoots, studded with pale buds.

One week later, over dinner, Pete says to me, "I found something else unexpected in the garden, and don't try to guess what it is."

"Well, what is it then?"

"There's another massive flower spike coming out of the yucca."

"Another one? But that's ridiculous. I've been out looking at it every evening. How can I not have noticed that?"

And we go outside, and there it is.

The unexpected pair grow bigger and bigger, and the buds burst into a myriad of white bell-shaped flowers, like small upside-down tulips, with a faint smell of oranges. The spears are taller than me, and taller than Pete—a good eight feet, and still increasing.

"I'm going to take a picture of this," he says, one evening. "But you'll have to be in it, to show the scale. I won't use flash. It will be an opportunity to try out the low-light capability on my new camera."

"You should be in it too," I say. "You could use your infra-red remote control thing."

So he bounds upstairs to fetch his equipment, and, returning to the garden, extends the legs of his tripod so that it perches gawkily on the lawn, and attaches the camera to its head.

"Now, stand as close as possible to the flower spikes, and look surprised."

I do my best to follow these instructions without getting a sword-shaped leaf in my neck. Pete fiddles with the settings, muttering to himself.

"It's really getting quite dark now," I say. "Do you think it's going to work?"

"It should be OK," he says abstractedly. "I've got an enormous high-quality engine. Right." He comes and stands behind me, putting his arms round my waist. "It's going to be a long exposure, so try not to move."

He presses the remote control device, and the camera responds with an opening "click." We stand there motionless for an interminable period, until we hear with relief the final "ker-lunk."

A few days later, having played with the file on the computer, Pete prints out the picture, and shows me. And there we are, enclosed within the muted greys and greens of twilight: me in hat, coat and boots, a pale face under a peaked brim, with a fixed and goofy smile; Pete, long and thin, in a zip-up cardigan, his features set in a quizzical expression. Beside us, monstrous yet beautiful, is a giant floral V-sign—in our case, sadly, not V for Victory, but at least for the time being, against all odds, two fingers stuck up at fate.

Since we stood together for our wedding photos, six years and ten months have passed. And what years—mottled, streaked and brindled like a complicated leopard, with alternate patches of despair and hope. My dark vow, as yet untested, is intact; I know now only how much harder it will be to keep.

Ending

I thought there'd be an ending to this story. Writing my final chapters I tried a new pill, and the initial results were good. I believed victory over the darkness would be the climax of my tale, an uplifting and satisfying denouement.

Life does not follow the narrative structures of Art. Corrupted by fiction, I anticipated change and plot development; I overlooked the awesome power of things to stay the same. The new pill took me on one more trip around my roundabout—I did not find the exit. In the teeth of every reasonable expectation, impossible lives, as I have found, endure.

These are the things that I have learnt:

The noblest truth is "There is suffering." The whole of history having been filled with such exotic and multifarious forms of it, "Why me?" is the question of an idiot. The sensible person says simply, "Why not?"

The great streams of human culture—literature, religion and philosophy—are wiser guides to living gracefully with suffering than modern pseudo-psychologies.

It is not possible to predict how people will respond

to chronic illness until it happens. Friends you thought you'd have for ever withdraw in puzzlement and distaste. Others, often quite unexpected others, set about the business of cheering you up, and stick to it, beautifully, for years.

Joy lurks in every mundane thing, just waiting to be found.

Love is impervious to reason.

And words are wonderful.

———

Author's Note

How do you write about having to live entirely in the dark? When I started in August 2010, well into my fourth extended period of total black, the result was not encouraging, reading, in broad terms, something like this:

Monday: stayed in dark
Tuesday: stayed in dark
Wednesday: stayed in dark

Even I, a novice, realised that as literature it lacked a certain vim.

Clearly I had to abandon the chronological approach—but what could I do instead? In the end, I wrote short sections, each focused on a different aspect of my dark life. So Part One draws on incidents from different periods that I spent in the black. In this state, time alters itself, becomes amorphous rather than linear;

you lose track of how long you've been in it, and you do not know if, this time, it will be for ever, or if or when you will ever get out.

In Part Two, the darkness begins to recede, but in a way that is partial and always temporary. I did not want to bore everybody by describing each of my slow climbs back towards the light. So I made a selection of the most significant and memorable steps.

For people interested in the actual order of events—maddening and frustrating as it was—I have included a diagram in the Appendix.

Many people have generously allowed me to write about them. Names and some details have been changed in order to protect privacy. I have taken the liberty of reconstructing conversations, to give a more complete sense of my experience, based on what I can remember regarding the sort of thing that was said. I did not know (thank goodness) what my future held, so I did not take contemporaneous notes.

Appendix

"What are you doing, darling? What's all this scrawl?"

"I'm trying to think of a way to set out all the ups and downs of my illness, without it getting completely boring and confusing."

"What you need," Pete says, "is a graph."

"A graph?"

"Yes. You've got two main variables—time and light sensitivity—and you plot one against the other."

"How do you mean?"

"Well, you put time as the abscissa—"

"The *what*?"

"The abscissa." He draws lines on my notebook. "And light tolerance as the ordinate."

"Do you mean the x coordinate and the y coordinate?"

"Yes—those are the mathematical names."

"Goodness," I say, getting excited, "I've never heard the word 'abscissa.'"

Pete is the only person I know who, though completely unpretentious and unassuming, will periodically use, in the course of everyday conversation, a word that is *entirely new to me*, and then stomp about insisting that he does not know what the fuss is about, and that whatever it is is a "perfectly normal word." I must confess I find this rather erotic.

So I plot time along the x-axis, and light tolerance along the y-axis, stack the different years on top of each other so the graph is not too long and thin, and the result is:

Fig. 1: Variation of light tolerance over time in one highly photo-sensitive female

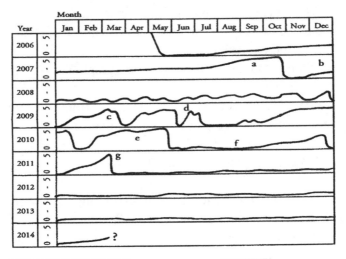

LEVEL OF LIGHT TOLERANCE

5 = curtains fully open downstairs,
    walks starting 1 hour before dusk
    and lasting 1 hour after dawn
0 = totally in the black

KEY EVENTS

a caravan holiday 1   e caravan holiday 3
b wedding   f started to write
c caravan holiday 2   this book
d Mottisfont   g increased steroid dose

Acknowledgements

Nina Milton made helpful and encouraging comments on the first draft. My mother read the next and gave it to her friend Babette, who gave it to her friend Anna Goodall, who passed it to Jane Finigan at Lutyens and Rubinstein. Jane wrote me a wonderful letter that stimulated me to expand it to the size of a proper book, and Jane is now my agent.

I would also like to thank Anna Steadman and Juliet Mahony at Lutyens and Rubinstein, David Forrer at Inkwell Management, Helen Garnons-Williams, Elizabeth Woabank and their team at Bloomsbury, and Bill Thomas, Kristine Puopolo and their team at Doubleday. Helen and Kristine formed a sensitive and rigorous editorial double act.

Eve, Lynda, Debbie, Dee, Jo and Ms. Edwards all typed various parts at various times, interpreting my curly handwriting and endless scrawled amendments.

My friends, family and telephone friends visited me, phoned me, wrote to me, made me laugh and kept me sane. My dear husband gave me more than words can possibly express.

ABOUT THE AUTHOR

Anna Lyndsey worked for several years in London as a civil servant until she became ill. She now lives with her husband in Hampshire. Anna is writing under a pen name.

231-3900